2023 Jefferson Nickel and Roosevelt Dime Error Coin Guide

Includes Buffalo Nickels and Mercury Dimes

By: Stan McDonald

Preface

Unsurpassed and comprehensive

Welcome to Jefferson Nickel and Roosevelt Dime Error Coin Guide for 2023. Included in this guide are Buffalo nickels and Mercury dimes.

Searching and discovering error coins can be a rewarding and profitable experience. There are thousands of coins in circulation with various error types. Some ways of locating error coins are searching through old collections, old rolls of coins, and boxes of coins from a local bankOld coin unopened rolls of coins have paper colored dark green or brown, and some rolls have the bank's name on the wrappers. Error coins found in rolls are restricted to the error types passing through coin rolling equipment. Error coin types that expand the size of the coin, such as off center and broadstruck coins, are usually located in mint boxes. Mint boxes that collectors can not purchase from the US Mint's online sales site can be purchased from companies with banking accounts with a Federal Reserve bank.

We welcome all questions about this guide and error coins. Contact us at: errorcoinexpert@aol.com

Listings in this book include:

• Die errors – Errors created from broken dies, cracked collars, hub errors, misaligned dies, doubled dies, and repunched mintmarks.
• Planchet Errors – Blanks used in the minting process with cracks, clips, defective, lamination, occluded gas, unplated, wrong metal, and wrong planchet.
• Striking errors – Errors created in the minting process such as broadstrikes, die caps, and others.

Error Coin Collecting

The popularity of error coin collecting has been increasing, evidenced by the growing number of error coins submitted to grading services. In 1999, PCGS started a new program to authenticate and encapsulate all types of error coins. PCGS noted, "February 22, 1999, NEWPORT BEACH, CALIF-A new grading, and authentication program for U.S. mint errors have been introduced by Professional Coin Grading Service (PCGS). Beginning immediately, PCGS will grade, authentic, and seal in their holders such mint errors as double strikes, capped die strikes, off-center strikes, off-metal planchets, broadstruck out-of-collar coins, and many other major mint errors."[1]

In 1999, a PCGS publication stated the following: "In the past, the grading and authentication of mint errors have been restricted to die varieties, such as a 1955 doubled die cent or the 1937-D 3-Legged Buffalo nickel," said Richard Montgomery, PCGS President. This new program will feature grading and authentication of mint errors created by mistakes made during the mint striking process. This new program will enable PCGS to certify some of the most spectacular striking errors in all of U.S. numismatics.[2] "

All encapsulating services coins are encasing error coins at record numbers. With so many error coin listings in this book, it would be a significant challenge to add photographs for all of them. Most error types are similar across the spectrum of U.S. coinage and presenting examples of modern-day errors should represent older coins.

Coin Specifications

---

[1] PCGS website
[2] PCGS website

Error coins with incorrect planchets, thin, thick, or the wrong alloy, can be identified using a weigh scale and comparing the data to the Mint specifications. The coin specifications are shown in the charts below from the US Mint website.[3] A collector can use a micrometer to measure the diameter and thickness of coins.

	Cent	Nickel	Dime
Denomination			
Composition	Copper Plated Zinc 2.5% Cu Balance Zn	Cupro-Nickel 25% Ni Balance Cu	Cupro-Nickel 8.33% Ni Balance Cu
Weight	2.500 g	5.000 g	2.268 g
Diameter	0.750 in. 19.05 mm	0.835 in. 21.21 mm	0.705 in. 17.91 mm
Thickness	1.52 mm	1.95 mm	1.35 mm
Edge	Plain	Plain	Reeded
No. of Reeds	N/A	N/A	119

	Quarter Dollar	Half Dollar	Dollar
Denomination			
Composition	Cupro-Nickel 8.33% Ni Balance Cu	Cupro-Nickel 8.33% Ni Balance Cu	Manganese-Brass 88.5% Cu 6% Zn 3.5% Mn 2% Ni
Weight	5.670 g	11.340 g	8.1 g
Diameter	0.955 in. 24.26 mm	1.205 in. 30.61 mm	1.043 in. 26.49 mm
Thickness	1.75 mm	2.15 mm	2.00 mm
Edge	Reeded	Reeded	Edge-Lettering
No. of Reeds	119	150	N/A

17A

Doubled Dies

Coins designated as doubled dies result from imperfect dies prepared from the master hub.[4] A steel rod is impressed on the master hub several times to create a working die for minting coins. Doubling occurs when there is a misalignment of the impressions on the die used in the

---

[3] US Mint website
[4] Hub – the tool used to create a die. It is the mirror image of a die in reverse.

minting process. Doubling can be classified as minor, medium or widespread.

2004-P Handshake DDO

Minor or medium doubling can be found on some Jefferson nickels. The 2004-P Jefferson nickel in the photo shows minor and medium spread doubling on the letters "TRUST" and the date.

Some DDO classifications are not well-published, leaving many error coins to circulate unchecked. There are eight doubled die classifications for error coins listed in Appendix A.

PCGS describes a doubled die as: "A die that has been struck more than once by a hub in misaligned positions, resulting in doubling of design elements. Before the introduction of hubbing, the individual elements of a coin's design were either engraved or punched into the die, so any doubling was limited to a specific element. With hubbed dies, multiple impressions are needed from the hub to make a single die with adequate detail. When shifting occurs in the alignment between the hub and the die, the die ends up with some of its features doubled – then imparts this doubling to every coin it strikes. The coins struck from such dies are called doubled-die errors"[5]

---

[5] PCGS – Definition for doubled die

RPM Error Coins

The photos in this book will help identify the modern-day error coins in circulation. Some RPM errors can be challenging to identify since the doubling is minor, and the errors often show a small, raised area around the mintmark or inside the mintmark.

1945-D/D RPM

The 1945 D over D Jefferson nickel has traces of the first mintmark.

Encapsulated Coins

The primary encapsulation services use standard numismatic descriptions for error coins like DDO and broadstruck. All of the grading services have identification numbers on their holders for authentication.

The NGC holder number is shown in the above photo, and a collector can enter the number into their online verification site.

The ANACS verification label is on the holder's reverse side, and they have a website for verifying the coin.

After the "/, " the last part of the PCGS number on the label is the number unique to the coin. PCGS has a website to enter the number for validation.

Some RPMs for specific dated coins have several different RPM errors, each noted on the holder provided by the grading service with a code they have adopted to recognize the error. It is difficult to compare one grading service RPM classification to another since they do not have an agreed standard for labeling the error. NGC uses its "variety plus" designation for coin errors and notes the error as VP-xxx. ANCS uses Coneca designations for repunched mintmarks and labels their holders as RPM-xx and other errors using the Fiaz-Stanton (FS) designation. PCGS uses the Fiaz-Stanton designation on their holders for error coins. Each of the three grading services mentioned uses error references from the same sources for coin types and denominations, such as Silver Dollars with the VAM designation.

Below are the three grading services labeling systems for the same error coin, a 1960 small over large date with an RPM.

1960 D/D SM/LG DATE 1C
VP-001
MS 66 RD

NGC VP-001 with small over large date notation

1960-D/D   1C
PCGS MS65RD
DDO FS-101 Sm/Lg Date
(FS-025.5)

PCGS DDO and FS-101

MS 64 RED
1960-D/D 1C   1392281
SM DT/LG DT FS-025.5

ANACS noting small over large date with the FS designation for the RPM

Collectors should look carefully at all encapsulated coins dating before 1999 when the coin services did not recognize error coins. Some of the oldest holders from the grading services do not have recognition for RPM errors since error encapsulation did not occur before 1999. [70]

Variations

Variations are not mint errors in the technical sense. Creating new hubs and dies that were not precisely like the original resulted in variations. In early U.S. coinage, there are coins in yearly mintages having multiple numbers of changes in date size, appearance, etc.

Some die variations are valuable, and others command no value difference with coin variations of the exact date and mintmark. Coins minted with die variations increase in value by the rarity of the number of coins minted.

Coin Grading

Grading coins is a subjective process, but there are standards for coins that are not in mint state condition and are widely accepted by the collecting community. PCGS has a website dedicated to grading coins available for anyone to use. The PCGS grading site has photos of coins in all grades collectors can use for comparisons.

Some circulated coins are borderline between one grade and another, especially those with weak obverse or reverse strikes. Dealers and grading services generally expand the grading for valuable coins by using more refined standards. These standards result in utilizing a numbering system for grading. A grade of "Fine" can become "F12" or "F15."

There are no agreed mint state grading standards with encapsulation services. Mint state grades range from MS60 through MS70, which complicates determining the grade of a coin. Coins graded by one service may not grade the same at another service, as evidenced by collectors sending coins to one service, then selecting another coin service and obtaining a different grade. Most coin dealers believe that PCGS is the toughest for grading coins, and PCGS coins usually command the most value. The most trusted encapsulation services are PCGS, NGC, and ANACS.

18C

The Environment

Coins stored in a moist or unclean environment will degrade with oxidation, develop carbon spots, and become discolored and pitted. Coins stored in the non-acid-free folders tend to attract carbon spots, pitting, and other distractions. To avoid surface damage to coins, use an acid-free coin album and holders. Placing a coin album in a zip-lock bag with desiccant will help keep the coins moisture-free.

19A

PCGS Defines Carbon Spots As:

"A spot mainly on copper and gold coins, though also occasionally found on U.S. nickel coins (which are 75 percent copper) and silver coins (which are 10 percent copper). Carbon spots are brown to black spots of oxidation ranging from minor to severe – some so large and far advanced the coin has no grade because of environmental damage."[6]

20A

Cleaning Coins

Cleaning a coin is never a good idea since it may reduce its value. There is no known method for cleaning copper coins without detection. One of the most common practices to clean a coin is whizzing, using a swirling brush with high-pressure water. Whizzing shows fine lines from the brushing that can be detected with close inspection. A cleaned copper coin is usually dull since the coin's luster denigrates in the cleaning process. Collectors should avoid any dull copper coin or a coin with a discolored surface.

---

[6] PCGS carbon spot – from the PCGS website

Nickels are rarely cleaned since the surface is more resilient, and collectors usually accept the toning. Many nickels are toned with red, amber, and blue tones, and some collectors seek these coins.

There is a process for cleaning silver coins known as dipping that removes the blackened surface from a coin and restores it to its original brilliance. Since overuse can remove the original luster, collectors should exercise care when using these chemicals.

The encapsulation services do encapsulate coins of value with issues. NGC, PCGS, and ANACS make notations on the holder, such as "cleaned," "damaged," "holed," and "scratched" when problems are recognized. PCGS also uses a no grade certification of "PCGS Genuine."

Best Coin Storage
Free of moisture
Clean, dry place free of chemicals.
PVC, acid-free coin folders
Encapsulated

Brilliant Uncirculated
PCGS defines BU as: "A generic term applied to any coin not circulated. Sometimes applied to Lincoln cent coins with little "brilliance" left, coins not brilliant are simply Uncirculated."

Coins in Circulation
Some publications purport a mint state coin has never been in circulation. The statement is incorrect since all MS coins other than those issued directly by the US Mint come from circulation in transactional change or bankrolls.

MS60

MS60 often indicates a coin with distractions that would otherwise grade higher value. Coins from dealers and collectors are graded as uncirculated versus the mint state grading system.

MS63 and MS64

Collectors and coin dealers often grade coins as brilliant or choice uncirculated for coins as MS63 and MS64. They are coins with a low value and are not of significant value to assign a mint state grade.

MS65 to MS67

The assigment of GEM uncirculated by collectors and dealers referes to coins in MS65 or higher grades.

Genuine

Some grading services use "genuine" to describe a damaged coin, including corrosion, scratches, nicks and cuts not given a grade. Coins not of significant value are rejected and not encapsulated.

Dealer Certification

Certified coin dealers are members of ANA and PNG.[7] PNG dealers must meet the following 5 provisions.

Applicant must:

1. Be at least 21 years of age and have five years' experience as a professional numismatist.
2. Have a net worth always of at least $250,000.
3. Agree by signature to abide by the PNG Code of Ethics.
4. Agree to submit to binding arbitration to settle any dispute relating to the purchase, sale, or trade of coins / numismatic items.

---

[7] PNG – Professionals Numismatist Guild

5. Provide a notarized statement from a certified public accountant that you meet or exceed the financial requirements of the PNG.[8]

Coin Collecting Tools

Many error coins slip by because the doubling or the RPM is not easily detectible. Having good tools augments the ability to discover error coins that would otherwise escape detection. New releases of coins from the US Mint allow collectors to discover an error coin in a high grade before the coin circulates.

NGC MS66 DDO

The coin in the photo would not have been discovered without a handheld microscope validating the doubling of the date and Liberty. The coin was discovered in bankrolled coins in 2021, two years after the coins were released into circulation.

---

[8] PNG Application – Taken from the PNG website

Die errors are the most common error in coins found in circulation. The most prevalent die errors are cracks, breaks, and partially missing details. Collectors and dealers do not usually seek coins with die cracks, and most of these coins are not offered as an error coins. Collectors usually overlook coins with die breaks unless they are BIE errors or cuds. While BIE errors are of low-value large cud errors can bring over $50 at auction. When the dies are damaged from abrasion, die polishing, or become filled with debris, some of the letters of numbers become faint or entirely missing on coins. There Missing letters and numbers are of low value, but some collectors seek these coins.

The Celestron or similar microscopes help detect some die errors that would otherwise be difficult to determine.

Celestron Microscope

Weight scale in grams or ounces

A weigh scale is handy for validating thin or think planchets, incorrect planchets, and wrong metals. A collector should weigh the 1983 Lincoln cents for those struck on bronze blanks.

Verifying thin and thick planchets using a caliper is the best method to determine any valuable variations. The standard thickness of a Lincoln cent is .0598 inches. Variations of a couple of hundredths are expected, especially since many coins are thicker on one side of the coin.
29A

Table of Contents

Chapter One - Major Error Categories, Coining Process, and Distribution

Major Error Categories
Die Errors
Die errors are created from broken dies, cracked collars, hub errors, misaligned dies, doubled dies, and repunched mintmarks.

Abrasions (scratches)
Bar
BIE
Broken hub
Broken punch
Collar break
Debris in hub
Die adjustment
Die breaks
Die crack
Die cud
Die cud retained
Die gouges
Die wear
Doubled die
Filled dies
Filled letters and numbers
Finned
Mintmark
Misaligned dies
Misplaced date
Missing details
Mule
Partial collar
Tilted collar

Mint Striking Errors

Mint striking errors result from the mint stamping process.

Bonded
Broadstrike
Brockage
Cancelled
Chain
Collar clash
Counter brockage
Cupped
Double denomination
Double struck
Extended rim
Flip over
Indent
Mated Pair
Multiple Struck
Off center
Reverse Brockage
Rotated
Saddle
Strick over
Strike through
Uniface

Planchet Errors

The coin blank and the blanks with upsets on edge are called planchets. A type I planchet is the coin blank itself. A type II planchet is the coin blank with the edging rolled on it. Planchet errors include blanks used in the minting process with cracks, clips, defective, lamination, occluded gas, unplated, wrong metal, and wrong planchet.

Blank
Clipped
Defective
Foreign

Fragmented
Improperly annealed
Lamination
Lamination retained
Occluded gas
Split
Thin/Thick
Tilted
Transitional
Unplated
Woodgrain
Wrong metal
Wrong planchet
30A

Die Creation

Die creation as described by the US Mint on their web site
www.USMINT.org is in detail below taken directly from
the US mint site word for word. A good understanding
minting process help the collector to understand how errors
occur.

"The process of making working dies begins by creating a
master hub. Making this master hub starts with a steel
blank. When the CNC milling machine cuts the coin design
into the end of the steel blank, it creates a "master" hub.
This process is repeated for a different design on a second
hub representing the design for the opposite side of the
coin.

The master hub is then used to create a "master die." Dies
start out as cylindrical steel blanks with a cone-shaped end.
After machining, the die blank moves down a conveyor to
the polishing machine.A robot-like arm picks up the
machined blank with a gripper that can load one blank into
the polisher while unloading another. The polishing
machine shines the cone end to a mirror-like finish.

Machinists measure the cone with a gauge before it continues to the inventory queue.

A working hub is formed. Each working hub creates batches of dies that strike the final circulating coins.

Most U.S. coin production starts with the arrival of coils—rolled-up strips of flat metal. Coils are about a foot wide, 1500 feet long, and about as thick as the final coin thickness. Each coil weighs close to 6,000 pounds.

How are blanks created?

A coil is hoisted onto a wheel that feeds into a blanking press. An operator cranks the wheel, so the end of the metal sheet goes into the blanking press through a slot on the side. From the sheet, the blanking press punches out round, plain-surfaced disks called cut blanks.

After cutting a batch of blanks, the remaining metal (webbing), is chopped off and collected in a bin. By recycling the webbing to make new coinage strip, we ensure material is not wasted. The blanks are now ready for the next steps: the creation of a planchet by softening, washing, and rimming the blanks' edges.

To soften the metal, blanks are placed in a furnace at temperatures over 700 degrees centigrade. Nickel blanks require the highest temperature. This process is called annealing during which, the molecules in the hard blanks are realigned to make the metal softer. The high temperature of the annealing process creates a grayish discoloration on the surface of the metal. To make it bright and shiny, the metal needs to be cleaned.

From the furnace, the blanks drop into a quench tank to reduce the temperature. Next, the blanks travel through a huge cylindrical tube called the whirlaway. Suspended high above the ground, these tubes tilt at a 45-degree angle toward the washing and drying station. As the blanks travel up the whirlaway toward the washer, excess liquid is drained.

After leaving the whirlaway, blanks are placed in a washing machine. Similar to the washing machine process you might have in your home, the blanks go through a series of cycles that soak and shake the blanks in various chemicals. This is to remove any oxides, tarnish, discoloration or contamination that remains after annealing.

Golden Dollars get a different treatment—they are burnished by steel shot resembling BBs.

The blanks are dried inside a tube and then poured out for the next treatment. In one hour, two tons of blanks can be annealed, washed, and dried.In addition, the raised rim helps protect the coin's design. The highest point of any coin design is always lower than the coin's rim. Raising the rim hardens the edge and helps keep the coin from eroding. This also helps the coins to stack

If a reeded[9] edge is required, it is applied to the planchet during coining by a collar inside the coining press. Reeded edges help to identify coin's denomination.

The next stage of production is coining. This is the process of adding the design to the planchet.

Planchets travel to the stamping press through a press feed system. Most presses are fed planchets transported directly from upsetting machines running the same denomination. Each row of stamping presses runs the same coin denomination (for example, nickels) with the press force adjusted to the strength of the metal. Sensors are able to screen and detect flawed planchets.

---

[9] Reeded edge – A coin that contains a series of impressions on the edge of the coin.

To strike the metal, one die (known as the anvil) is held motionless and the other die (known as the hammer) strikes the planchet's surface. The anvil is usually a reverse (or tails) die and the hammer is the obverse (or heads).
The planchet's size, hardness, design intricacy, and relief determine the force needed to strike. Golden Dollar coins require the greatest force, and pennies require the least force.

Fast-paced presses churn out 750 new coins every minute. The coins fill a collection box called a trap. An inspector checks the coins to see if they meet United States Mint quality standards.

Coins are compared to both visual and fill standards. Next, critical Statistical Process Control (SPC) and capability quality data are entered into the United States Mint's data collection system to track key processes.
If the coins pass inspection, the operator pulls the trap's lever. This discharges the coins onto a conveyor belt that transports them to the counting and bagging area.
An automatic counting machine, fitted with a sensor that detects correct products, counts the coins and drops them into large bags.

12A

Six steps of the minting process for U.S. coins from the U.S. Mint

"Step 1: Blanking: The U.S. Mint buys strips of metal approximately 13 inches wide and 1,500 feet long to manufacture the nickel, dime, quarter, half-dollar, and the dollar. The metal strips come rolled in a coil. Each coil is fed through a blanking press, which punches out round discs called blanks. The leftover strip, called webbing, is shredded, and recycled. To manufacture pennies, the Mint buys ready-made planchets after supplying fabricators with copper and zinc.

Step 2: Annealing, Washing, and Drying: The blanks are heated in an annealing furnace to soften them. Then they are run through a washer and dryer.

Step 3: Upsetting: The blanks go through an upsetting mill. Upsetting raises a rim around their edges, turning the blanks into planchets.

Step 4: Striking: Finally, the planchets go to the coining press. Here, they are stamped with the designs and inscriptions making them genuine United States legal tender coins.

Step 5: Inspection: A press operator uses a magnifying glass to spot-check each batch of new coins.

Step 6: Counting and Bagging: An automatic counting machine counts the coins and drops them into bags. The bags are sealed, loaded on pallets, and taken by forklifts to be stored. New coins are shipped by truck to Federal Reserve Banks. From there, the coins go to your local bank.[10]

Distribution of coins and notes

"Currency notes and coins are all produced by the Treasury Department. After production, the Treasury ships the coins and currency notes' directly to Federal Reserve banks and branches. The Federal Reserve then releases them as required by the commercial banking system. The demand for money by the public varies from day to day and from week to week. There are even differences from season to season. Banks are usually first to feel the impact of the public's demand for cash. To meet the public's needs, banks turn to their regional Federal Reserve bank for coins and currency when their supplies are low.[11]

"Coin Distribution, too, assures the smooth and sufficient flow of coins; the United States Mint continually revises its techniques for estimating coinage demands. In planning

---

[10] US Mint website
[11] US Mint website

production and scheduling coin shipments, the United States Mint uses long-range economic indicators and historical seasonal trends such as Christmas to decide how many coins to manufacture."[12]

"Forecasting coin demand is difficult. Estimates must also include an amount enough to provide an inventory that would absorb any deviation. Armored carriers usually transport ten-cent coins, quarter-dollar coins, and half-dollar coins, while tractor-trailer trucks transport one-cent coins and five-cent coins.[13]"

"Federal Reserve banks arrange in advance to receive new coin shipments for the coming year. They do this in amounts and on a schedule to maintain their inventories at the required levels. Under this arrangement, the United States Mint can schedule its production schedule efficiently. Even with planning, there are occasions when coin shortages arise. The Federal Reserve banks must follow the advance shipping schedules. Except in an emergency, there are no provisions for obtaining additional coins.[14]"

"Federal Reserve banks receive coins at face value because they are obligations of the United States Government. The Banks store the coins until they need to fill orders from the commercial banks in their district. The Federal Reserve banks fill these orders from their vault stocks of both new and circulated coins. Also, they fill the orders without regard to date or mintmark. Coin shipments leave the Federal Reserve banks by armored car, registered mail, or express.[15]"

---

[12] US Mint website
[13] US Mint website
[14] US Mint website
[15] US Mint website

"If a commercial bank has excess coins on hand, they may return the coins to the Federal Reserve bank. It then sorts the coins for fitness. They return badly worn or bent coins to the United States Mint, which melts them down and makes them into new coins. Also, the banks remove foreign and counterfeit coins from circulation. According to Federal Reserve sources, over 20 billion coins valued at well over $2 billion passes through their coin processing units each year."[16]

---

[16] US Mint website

Chapter Two – History of Buffalo Nickels, Jefferson Nickels, Mercury Dimes and Roosevelt Dimes

Buffalo Nickel Specifications 1913 to 1938
Weight 5 grams
Diameter .835 inches
Thickness 1.95 mm

Jefferson Nickel Specifications 1938 to date
Weight 5 grams
Diameter .835 inches
Thickness 1.95 mm

Mercury Dime Specifications 1914 to 1945
Weight 2.5 grams
Diameter .705 inches
Thickness 1.35 mm

Roosevelt Dime Specifications 1946 to date
Weight 2.268 grams
Diameter .705 inches
Thickness 1.35 mm

Nickels
The nickel alloy used to mint coins is strong and resilient. Although coins with nickel alloys can wear, the Jefferson nickel holds up for 50 plus years before enduring extensive wear.

The name "nickel" is not representative of the five-cent piece since it comprises mainly copper. The Jefferson nickel consists of 75% copper and 25 % nickel, a blended alloy that is not clad coated.

During World War II, the Mint changed the nickel content to 56% copper, 35% silver, and 9% manganese. The nickels range from 1942 through 1945, and they have a "large" mintmark above the dome on the reverse, which identifies them. Both designs were minted in 1942.

The first nickel entered production in 1866. Although the shield nickel had a beautiful design, the Mint could not maintain the dies for the finer details. Mint workers manually performed sharpening the die details during this period which led to countless variations. The shield nickel mintages began in 1866 and ended in 1883.

The Liberty nickel was less of a design challenge for the Mint to produce. The Liberty nickel carries the nickname of "V" nickel because there is a roman numeral on the reverse side indicating five cents. Liberty nickel minting began in 1883 and ended in 1913.

In 1913, the first Buffalo nickel circulated. "According to artist James E. Fraser[17], the Native American on the Indian Head and Buffalo nickels was actually a combined image created from three people: a Cheyenne named Chief Two Moons, an Iroquois named Chief John Big Tree, and a Sioux named Chief Iron Tail.[18]" The series ended with the last production in 1938, coinciding with the Jefferson nickel mintages.

The highest point on the Buffalo nickel was the date, and it wore off the coin quickly, leaving thousands of dateless coins circulating. Thousands of buffalo nickels circulated in the 1950s and 1960s with partial or no dates.

---

[17] James Fraser is the Mint designer for the Buffalo nickel.
[18] US Mint archives

During the mintages of the Buffalo nickel, the Mint used dies with a two and a three feather portrait. The two feather mintages are the lowest. The Buffalo nickel series is one of the most difficult to collect because of low mintages in some dates and mintmarks.

The Jefferson nickel is the only United States coin with significant quantities in circulation from the 1950s. The lowest mintages are with the first two years of mintages from San Francisco and Denver and the 1950-D. Except for the war nickel series, the nickel was the only metal currency not to be impacted by hoarding or removed for silver content, the coins circulated freely in the 1970s. Most of the error coins are RPMs due to Mint workers reworking the die.

The earliest mintages of Jefferson nickels were minted with little step detail even though the coin's design included five steps on Monticello. The nickel's hardness made it difficult to refine the die-making process to show full steps on coins minted. Some dies may not have been prepared with the full steps due to poor die preparation. The dies also wore down quickly, and millions of coins had partial or no step design. A full step nickel must have completed lines without bag marks and nicks that often interrupt the step lines.

There are dates that the primary coin services have not graded Jefferson nickels with full steps in any significant quantity. The lowest mintages with graded complete steps are the 1953 and S, 54 S mintages, 1960, 1961 and1961-D issues, the 1963-D issue, the 1965 issue, the 1966 issue, the 1967 issue, the entire 1969 series minted in Denver, and San Francisco, and finally the 1970-D mintage. The US Mint refined the die-making process in 1971. The mintages of coins with full steps were abundant after 1971, and the continued refinement of the coin's reverse led to increasing the steps from five to six.

2006 Jefferson nickel

In 2004 and 2005, the Mint issued the Westward Journey series designs, including the Peace Medal and Keelboat, Ocean View, and Bison nickel designs. Although none of these designs are rare, there is a lot of hoarding, making these coins somewhat scarce. The Mint changed the portrait's design in 2006 to a larger head of Jefferson, and it remains the design today.

About Felix Schlag, the Jefferson Nickel Designer

Congress approved a new nickel design with the portrait of Thomas Jefferson. The initials FS is found on all Jefferson nickel mintages. Below are excerpts from www.FelisSchlag.com, a website dedicated to him.

"Felix Oskar Schlag

(September 4, 1891 - March 9, 1974)

Born in Frankfurt am Main (Frankfurt on the Main River), Germany to Carl (Karl) Friedrich Schlag and Therese Josephine (Fischer) Schlag, Felix Schlag would come to the United States in 1929 and achieve national fame in 1938 for his winning design of the Jefferson nickel." [19]

"Jefferson Nickel Competition

(January 25, 1938 - April 15, 1938)

Many accounts of the origin of the Jefferson Nickel seem content to state that when the Indian Head or Buffalo nickel reached the end of its 25-year statutory required minimum life the United States Treasury held a design competition and Felix Schlag's submittal was selected from some 398 entrants."[20]

Mercury Dimes

Ron Guth wrote an article published by PCGS that describes the history of the Mercury dime. "In 1916, a new Dime design was introduced to replace the old Barber design that had been in use since 1892. Designed by A.A. Weinman, the new design featured a portrait of Liberty facing left, wearing a winged cap. Because of the resemblance to the Roman god, Mercury, the coin became known popularly as the "Mercury Head" Dime. The reverse blends a Roman fasces (ax surrounded by a tied bundle of sticks) and an olive branch, indicating America's military

---

[19] www.felixschlag.com
[20] www.felixschlag.com

readiness but also their desire for peace. The Mercury Head Dime series is one of the most popular in all of American numismatics. Apart from the 1916-D and 1942 overdates, most dates can be obtained with little difficulty. However, several of the dates are extremely rare in high grade. The most desirable issues are those with Full Split Bands on the reverse, which means all of the bands that hold the fasces together on the reverse must be clearly and completely separated. While much attention is focused on the central bands, the bands on the ends of the fasces must be separated, as well. Again, many dates are extremely rare in Gem condition with Full Split Bands.[21]"

Roosevelt Dimes
The Roosevelt dime design has not changed much since the first issue in 1946. Congress authorized the US Mint to design and issue the Roosevelt dime in 1946, replacing the Mercury dime. The US Mint describes the obverse and reverse of the Roosevelt dime signed by John Sinnock as follows:

"Obverse (heads): First appeared in 1946, soon after the death of President Franklin Roosevelt. The Roosevelt dime was released on the late president's birthday, January 30. The design features Roosevelt's left-facing bust.
Reverse (tails): Displays a torch signifying liberty with an olive branch on the left signifying peace and an oak branch on the right signifying strength and independence.[22]"

John Sinnock was the designer of the <u>Roosevelt dime</u> and <u>Franklin half dollar</u>, among other U.S. coins. His initials can be found at the base of the Roosevelt and Franklin busts. He also sculpted, although did not design, the <u>Purple</u>

---

[21] Ron Guth -PCGS contributor
[22] US Mint website

Heart medal, the Yangtze Service Medal, and various other medals and commemorative coins.

"Sinnock was born July 8, 1888, in Raton, New Mexico, and was educated at the Philadelphia Museum School of Industrial Art. He won the A.W. Mifflin Award for study abroad. Sinnock was well-traveled. His longtime confidant was Margaret Campbell who inherited much of his artwork as well as his personal collection of materials related to the development of the Roosevelt Dime.

For ten years Sinnock was an art instructor at both his alma mater and at Western Reserve University. He was appointed Assistant Engraver and Medalist at the Philadelphia Mint in 1917 before becoming the Chief Engraver in 1925[23]"

From 1946 through 1964, Roosevelt dimes contained 90 percent silver, making them more valuable for the silver content in circulated condition by the mid-1960s. In 1965, the Roosevelt dime changed to a copper center with nickel plating to reduce the cost of minting dimes.

The Roosevelt dime is the only U.S. coin series that has not changed its design since 1946. Even when most U.S. coinage designs changed in 1976 to display 1776-1976, the dime remained unchanged. The only change made to the coin was adding a "P" in 1980 to the coin's obverse.

---

[23] "John R. Sinnock, Coin Designer". *The Numismatic Scrapbook Magazine*: pg. 260. March 15, 1946.

Chapter Three – Error Definitions

231

Abrasions (die error)

Scratches on the die create raised scattered lines on the surface, lettering, and numbering on a coin.

1998-P Jefferson Nickel

Ball Serif

The top of the "S" mintmark has a thick round area appearing like a ball.

1945-S Lincoln cent

Bar Die Break (die error)

A die break over the tops of the lettering on a coin appears like a bar.

1960 Jefferson nickel

Basining – The process of polishing dies before the minting process which can lead to details on parts of the coin that are not raised to the proper height.

Basining could be the root cause of the 1943 cents with a lightly struck four and mintmark, although not proven[24].

"BIE" errors (die error) A die break between the "B" and the "E" is a BIE error. The material between the letters can vary in size and length.

1994 Lincoln cent

Blank (planchet error)
A blank is the metal disk punched out of sheet stock used for coin minting. A type I planchet is the metal disk without edging. A type II planchet has a rolled edge.

---

[24] Many numismatic experts attribute basining to lightly struck letters on the 1943 Lincoln cents. Since the US Mint does not confirm minting issues, collectors are left to determine the most likely cause.

Type I   Type II

Bonded Pair (striking error)

Two or more blanks enter the minting chamber are struck together as one piece are bonded pairs.

1998 Jefferson nickels – bonded pair

Broadstrike (striking error)

A coin struck without the collar holding it in place results in the coin expanding under the pressure of the dies. Broadstrikes are often combined with other error types such as uncentered, struck out of the collar, and double struck.

1998 Jefferson nickel

Broadstruck and cupped

Brockage (striking error)

PCGS definition: "A brockage is a Mint error, an early capped die impression where a sharp incused image has been left on the next coin fed into the coining chamber. Most brockages are partial; full brockages are rare and the most desirable form of the error.[25]"

Broken Hub (die error)

---

[25] PCGS website

When a hub is damaged from debris, or rework the details are often missing or not the intended height. A die made from a damaged hub may be missing details or not at the intended height.

2004 Lincoln cent

Broken Punch (die error)
A punch used to create a mintmark is partially broken, resulting in missing details.

Notch on the bottom left

Cancelled Planchet – Waffle (striking error)
The mint destroys coins, not meeting standards by crushing the coin.

Canceled Jefferson nickel

Chain Strike (striking error)

A chain strike occurs when two planchets enter the minting chamber side by side and are struck by the minting dies.

1973-D Chain struck and off center

Circles (die error)
There is no known information identifying the root cause of small circles on some coin issues, especially Jefferson nickels. The circles are created in the minting process from a die that has been compromised.

Jefferson nickel with a circle

Clipped Planchets (planchet error)
There are several types of clipped planchet errors. Some planchet errors can be severe, with most of the planchet missing. Classifications include clipped planchets, curved clips, bowtie clips, assay clips, and others.

1920 Clipped planchet

Collar Break (die error)

When the collar breaks, the planchet shifts during the minting process, creating a thicker rim on one side of the coin. Some collar breaks are more extreme than others, with flattened areas extending outside the expected diameter of the coin.

1943 Jefferson nickel – collar break

Collar Clash (striking error)

A collar clash occurs when the striking die is not lined up correctly, and the die strikes the collar. The features on the collar, sometimes a reeded edge, are transferred to the die. Subsequent coins minted will have the reeded edge impressions on the surface of the rim.

1974 Washington Quarter

Clashed Dies (die error)
See die clash

Concentric lath lines (die error)
A damaged die shows lath lines from mint workers refining the die.

Counter brockages (striking error)
A previously struck coin and capped die is a "counter brockage." The capped die strikes a coin already struck, and the obverse design is impressed into the cap. The result will be a design where the cap face will be an incuse[26] brockage.

---

[26] Merriam-Webster - formed by stamping or punching in -used chiefly of old coins or features of their design

Counter Brockage

Cupped Strike (striking error)
A broadstruck coin that is curved downward is a cupped strike. A capped die is similar, but the coin is not expanded.

1997-P Jefferson nickel cupped and broadstruck

Debris in Hub (Die Error)
A coin with debris in the hub transferred to a working die shows as a bold, thick line on the coin's surface.

1983 Lincoln cent

Defective Planchet (Planchet Errors)
A defective planchet refers to a split, cracked, or missing piece(s) on the blank before the coining process.

Defective planchet

Die Adjustment Strikes (die error)
Adjustments to the pressure in the coining press result in coins being weakly struck.

Die adjustment

Die Cap (striking error)
A "die cap" error results from a coin getting stuck on a die and being struck several times. The hammer or anvil die will eventually take the shape of the cap, and subsequent coins show deep impressions. There are different die cap stages, from blurred coinage to coinage, with most details present.

Die cap

Die Chip (die error)

Die chip occurs when the die is damaged, and small irregular raised metal areas to appear, usually around the inside of letters and numbers. (see filled letters and numbers)

Die chips on portrait

Die Clash (die error)

A coin minted with traces of the reverse on the obverse, or the opposite is a "die clash" error. Die clash errors result from the minting dies pressed together without a planchet between them - one die imprints with the details of the other side of the die. In subsequent stampings, the coins minted contain some reverse or obverse details on opposite sides of the coin.

1970-D Lincoln cent die clash

Die Crack (die error)
The mint die incurs a fracture or break. The crack in the die fills with metal from the stamping process, leaving a raised line of various lengths, sometimes branching into several areas on the coin.

2020 Lincoln cent

Die Cud– Broken Die (die error)
A piece of the die breaks away forming a cud.

1959 Jefferson nickel

Die Cud – Retained (die error)

A retained cud occurs when a piece of the die breaks but is held in place by the collar.

Retained Die Cud

Die Deterioration Doubling

Die deterioration doubling (DDD) occurs when the dies wear, or the die is improperly hardened for use. The doubling shows material around the letters and numbers.

Lincoln cent

Die Gouges (die error)

Short, thick, raised lines or bumps on the surface of a coin result from gouges in a die. Die gouges are caused by a die that has been deeply scratched or gouged by foreign material.

1986 Lincoln cent

Die Scratches (see Abrasions)

Die Wear (die error)
Extensive die wear reduces or eliminates the details on the coin.

1999 State Quarter

Double Denomination (striking error)
A coin struck on another denomination previously minted results in a double denomination.

Lincoln cent struck on a Roosevelt dime

Doubled dies (die error)
Coins designated as doubled dies result from imperfect dies prepared from the master hub. Dies are impressed on the master hub several times to create a working die for minting coins. Doubling occurs when there is a misalignment of the impressions.

1972 doubled die

PCGS describes as doubled die as: *"A die that has been struck more than once by a hub in misaligned positions, resulting in doubling of design elements. Before the introduction of hubbing, the individual elements of a coin's design were either engraved or punched into the die, so any doubling was limited to a specific element. With hubbed dies, multiple impressions are needed from the hub to make a single die with adequate detail. When shifting occurs in the alignment between the hub and the die, the die ends up with some of its features doubled – then imparts this doubling to every coin it strikes. The coins struck from such dies are called doubled-die errors"*[27]

Double Struck (striking error)
See also multiple struck
A double-struck coin results when a coin remains in the minting chamber and is struck again with the dies.

Extended Rim (striking error)

---

[27] PCGS – Definition for doubled die

The coin is not seated correctly in the minting chamber, leaving the upset rim from the rolling process intact.

Lincoln cent

Filled Dies (die error)
Dies filled with metal, grease, or debris produce weakly struck coins.

Filled dies

Filled Letters and Numbers (die errors)
A die chipping away around letters and numbers fills around the details.

1955-S Lincoln cent

Finned Rim (collar error)
Die misalignment splits the blank's upset away from the minted coin. Extreme finning occurs when the upset portion of the blank peels away.

Lincoln cent – finned rim

Flip Over Strike (striking error)
A coin minted on one side flips over in the minting chamber and is struck again.

Flip over

Fold Over Strike (striking error)
A minted coin re-entering the minting chamber on edge is crushed flat.

No date Lincoln cent fold over strike

Foreign Planchet (Planchet Errors)
A planchet designated for foreign currency enters the minting chamber and is minted with the US dies.

Lincoln cent

Fragment (planchet error)
A fragment is a piece of metal intended as scrap but minted as a coin.

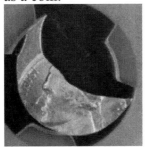
Cresent struck on a fragment

Improperly Annealed (planchet error)
Planchets that are not adequately softened for minting are improperly annealed. The minted coins often appear with a red tint.

1977 Eisenhower dollar

Indent (striking error)

Another planchet enters the minting chamber, and it is crushed into the coin.

2000 Lincoln cent

Inverted Mintmark (see mintmark errors)

Lamination Error (planchet errors)
A piece of the planchet is weakened when struck and either fully or partially detaches from the coin.

1943-P Jefferson nickel lamination

Lamination Error - Retained (Planchet Errors)
Retained lamination occurs when the planchet, which peels away, remains intact on the coin's surface.

Retained lamination

Machine Doubled

Machine doubling is a thin flat area surrounding the letters or numbers on the intended design. The US Mint states, "Machine doubling, which is also known as strike, ejection, shelf or shift doubling, is not the result of the design on the die being doubled. Instead, this type of doubling occurs when the die strikes a planchet. If the die is not correctly seated, it can move slightly or bounce during the moment of striking, creating a flat, shelf-like doubling. This effect will be different on all coins struck, so it is technically not a variety but rather more of a striking error.[28]"

Mated Pairs (striking error)

When two coins are struck together and located in the Mint box, they are deemed mated pairs.

1996 mated pair

Mintmark Errors (die error)

Dual Mintmarks

Dual mintmarks occur when a mint worker does not entirely remove the first mintmark and then adds another mintmark to the die.

---

[28] NGC website

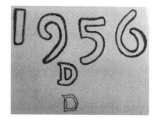

Horizontal mintmark

The first mintmark is misplaced, and a Mint worker fails to remove all details.

Inverted Mintmark

An inverted mintmark occurs when a mint worker hammers a mintmark in a die upside down.

Over mintmark – OMM

PCGS definition: "A coin struck with a die on which one mintmark is engraved over a different mintmark.[29]"

---

[29] PCGS website

Phantom Mintmark

The mintmark is not entirely removed, leaving small traces on the die.

RPM

The first mintmark is not entirely removed from the die.

D/D mintmark

Rotated mintmark

A rotated mintmark is tilted to the left or right of the standard placement.

Tilted mintmark
A mintmark punched into a die on an angle results in
tilting. The top portion of the mintmark is thick, and it is
tapered toward the bottom, often missing some portions at
the bottom.

Misaligned Dies (die error)
When the hammer, the anvil, and the collar dies are not
aligned correctly, coins are minted with rims that vary in
width around the coin.

1970-D Lincoln cent

Misplaced Date (die error)
The date is incorrectly positioned on the die.

1866 half dollar

Missing Clad Layer
The clad layer is not added to the planchet, making the coin slightly underweight and miscolored.

Washington quarter

Missing Details (die error)
Missing letters and lack of detail are attributed to die wear, die abrasions, and filled dies.

199x Lincoln cent

Mule Error (die error)
A mule error occurs when obverse details are of one coin, and the reverse is of another coin.

Lincoln cent planchet with a dime reverse.

Multiple Struck (striking error)
A jammed coin in the minting chamber may get struck three, four, five, or more times before it is ejected.

Multiple struck and indented

Occluded Gas (Planchet Errors)
Bubbles appear on the coin's surface caused by gas trapped during the plating process.

1982-D Lincoln cent

Off Center (striking error)

A coin struck on a blank that was not adequately centered over the anvil, or lower, die.[30]

1980-D Jefferson nickel

Over Mintmark OMM (see mintmark errors)

Partial Collars (die error)
A planchet fed into the minting chamber is stuck outside the collar, resulting in an uneven rim around the coin. The portrait and the letting on the coin are shifted to one side of the coin.

1914 Buffalo

Partial Collar Tilted (striking error)
A coin entering the minting chamber struck on an angle with a cracked or moving collar results in a slope on one side of the coin.

---

[30] PCGS website

1944 Lincoln cent

Phantom Mintmark (see mintmark errors)

Reverse Brockage – (striking error)
A reverse brockage error has the portrait in the reverse direction.

Rotated – (striking error)
The dies are not aligned correctly, leading to a rotated coin.

1975 Lincoln cent rotated

Saddle-struck – (striking error)

Saddle-struck coins occur in a multi-press operation when the coin straddles two presses. Both presses stamp the coin while the coin bends between misaligned dies.

Lincoln cent

Split Planchet (Planchet Errors)
Part of the planchet is missing before striking or the planchet breaks apart in the minting chamber.

Split before the strike

Split after the strike

Spread (striking error)
Spread is the degree of doubling on a coin. The spread is wide, medium, or small.[31]

Doubled "LIBERTY", with a "wide" spread.

Doubled "LIBERTY" with "medium" spread.

PCGS MS66 DDO[32]

A small spread of doubling on a coin reveals minor overlapping of letters and numbers.

Strike through – (striking error)

Debris enters the minting chamber and is pressed into the coin, causing the details to be wholly or partially blurred. Extreme cases involve paper clips, staples, and other objects impressed into the coin.

Struck through cloth

---

[31] There is no standard for the terminology used to describe the breadth of the error.

[32] Discovered by the author

Wire or other foreign object struck into the coin

Struck through debris

Retained strike through

Strike Over (striking error)

A strike-over occurs when a previously minted coin enters the minting change and is struck by a die set up for a different denomination.

Lincoln cent

Thin/Thick Planchets (planchet error)

When a planchet is thin or thick, the coin becomes lighter or heavier than intended.

Tilted Mintmark (see mintmark errors)

Transitional – (Planchet Errors)
A transitional error refers to minting a coin on discontinued planchet stock from the prior year. Examples are a 1983 Lincoln cent minted on a copper planchet and a 1943 cent minted on a copper planchet.

Uniface – (striking error)
A coin planchet enters the minting chamber over a planchet already in the minting chamber. The planchets struck together, leaving one side blank.

Uniface Lincoln cent

Unplated – (Planchet Errors)
The weight of a normal Lincoln-copper plated zinc cent is 2.5 grams. Any coin missing the plating should weigh slightly under 2.5 grams. It is possible to remove the plating from copper-zinc coins chemically. Caution – BU examples of unplated cents will have luster. Removing the

plating of a BU cent will dull the coin's surface.

1983 Lincoln cent with no copper plating[33] The coin appears to be zinc colored.

Variations

Variations are intentional differences in mintages of the same year. The most notable variety for the Lincoln cent series is 1909 with and without the V.D.B. The mint began minting 1909 coins with the large designer initials and then removed the initials during the mintage.

Until 1992, the U.S. Mint manufactured cents with the "wide" AM. All 1993 and after, issues were intended to have a close AM for circulation. Coins have been discovered with wide A.M.s dated 1992 and 1993. There are coins dated 2000 with close A.M.s in circulation.

All proof Lincoln Cents issued from 1993 to 2009 should have the AM of America separated from one another.

1999-S Close and Wide AM

Wood-Grained – (planchet error)

A wood-grained Lincoln cent has stripes, covering the obverse or reverse of the coin.

1983 Lincoln cent

Wrong Planchet – (planchet error)

A coin struck on a different planchet than intended is considered a wrong planchet.

Lincoln cent struck on dime planchet

231

Chapter Four – Nickel Errors 1913-Date

Buffalo Nickel 1913-1938

1923 buffalo nickel

The buffalo nickel design ended the liberty design on U.S. coinage for nickels. The nickel beginning in 1913, featured an American Indian on the obverse and a buffalo on the reverse. Inherent in the design, the date was the high point of the coin and subject to wear off the surface—consequently, millions of Buffalo nickels circulated in the 1960s without visible dates. The Mint also used two different obverses for some coinage dates showing a two feather and a three-feather design

The best-known error coin in the buffalo nickel series is the three-legged buffalo dated 1937-D. In 1937, refurbishing the die used to produce the coin continued until the leg wore off the die. A second Buffalo nickel struck with 3 ½ legs is not well known, the 1913 issue. A small number of 1936-D and 1937-D Buffalo nickels designated as 3 ½ legs reside in holders.

1937-D 3-legged buffalo

The mint produced two versions of the 1913 buffalo nickel intentionally. One version portrays the buffalo on a mound, and the second version shows the buffalo on flat ground. Collectors refer to these coins as type one and type two versions with mintages from Philadelphia, Denver, and San Francisco. Both versions are easy to recognize since there is a distinct difference between the mound and flat ground issues.

Buffalo nickel type 2 flat ground.

Buffalo Nickels
Clipped Planchets
1913-S 4% (MS64, $300)
1918 (MS61, $140)

1919 4%, w/broadstruck (MS66, $1,785)
1919 w/partial collar (MS64, $150)
1919 curved (AU53, $750) (MS64, $1,495)
1919 double (AU58, $345)
1919 straight, w/20% off center (MS61, $1,380)
1920 2% (AU58, $375)
1920-S (MS62, $355-$635)
1921-S w/flaw (MS60, $995)
1924 4% (MS64, $345)
1925-S (AU55, $200)
1927 6% (MS64, $225)
1928-S ragged 14% (MS61, $165)
1935 2% (AU55, $60) (MS63, $100)
1935 3% (F15, $25) (MS62, $50)
1935 5% (MS64, $100) (MS65, $275)
1935 double 4% (MS64, $300)
1936 1% (MS64, $70-$180)
No date (AU53, $130) (MS64, $575)
No date elliptical (MS66, $150)

Buffalo Nickels
Cracked and Defective
1926-S cracked (XF45, $705-$940) 2022
1938-D cracked (MS65, $180) 2022

Buffalo Nickels
Cuds and Retained Cuds
1913 25% reverse (AU53, $170-$405)
1917-S 25% (EF40, $175)
1918-D 25% EF45, $210)
1919-D 25% retained, obverse (MS60, $460-$635)
1919-D retained, obverse (MS61, $460)
1920 25% obverse and reverse (VG8, $115)
1920 25% reverse (G6, $145) (AU50, $920)
1935 25% reverse (F15, $275)
No date (no grade, $70-$260)

Buffalo Nickels
Die Clash
1913-S (AU55, $385)

Buffalo Nickels
Doubled Dies
1913 DDO, buffalo on flat ground (MS63, $435) (MS64, $235)
1913 DDR, buffalo on flat ground (MS62, $335-$515) (MS63, $430)
1913 DDR, buffalo on mound (MS62, $1,800)
1916 DDO (VG8, $5,300-$7,500) (VG10, $7,050) (F15, $975-$6,600) (VF25, $5,885) (VF35, $11,425) (XF40, $16,800) (XF45, $17,825-$22,425) (AU50, $25,875) (AU58, $46,000-$49,350) (MS63, $105,000) (MS64, $172,000-$264,500)
1917 DDO (XF40, $505) (MS63, $2,040)
1917 DDR (MS64, $10,925)
1918 DDR (VG10, $235)
1927-S DDO (VF35, $94) (XF40, $505)
1929 DDO (MS65, $660)
1930 DDO (MS64, $165-$590) (MS66, $630)
1930 DDR (VF35, $140) (AU50, $115) (MS65, $750-$2,500)
1934 DDO (AU50, $315)
1935 DDR (F12, $30-$40) (VF20, $110-$210) (VF25, $276) (VF30, $140-$280) (AU55, $1,500-$2,530) (AU58, $2,520-$4,600) (MS61, $7,185) (MS62, $5,175) (MS63, $11,500) (MS64, $6,900-$16,100) (MS65, $25,300)
1935-S DDO (AU58, $430)
1936 DDO (VF20, $65) (AU55, $135-$140) (MS63, $110-$560) (MS64, $995-$1,000) (MS65, $1,080) (MS66, $3,840) 2022

Buffalo Nickels
Fragment
No date w/split (MS63, $750)
No date w/lamination, reverse (MS63, $750) 2022

Buffalo Nickels
Lamination
1913-D reverse (VF20, $130)
1913-D (F15, $100)
1913-S (MS65, $315)
1913-S buffalo on flat ground (XF40, $50)
1913-S buffalo on raised ground (F12, $185) (XF40, $210) (AU50, $520)
1913-S buffalo on raised ground, obverse (XF40, $235)
1914-D (XF40, $70)
1914-D obverse (F12, $55)
1914-D reverse (MS64, $355)
1914-S (VF30, $35)
1915-D (AU55, $105)
1915-D obverse (MS62, $140)
1915-S obverse (AU55, $310) (AU58, $345)
1916 (VG8, $95)
1916-D (XF40, $40) (AU55, $200) (MS61, $75) (MS63, $80)
1916-S (AU50, $40)
1917-S (MS61, $390) (MS62, $275) (MS64, $490)
1918-D (XF45, $80)
1918-D obverse (MS64, $295-$950)
1918-D reverse (MS63, $515-$635)
1918-S (AU50, $155) (XF45, $105) (AU58, $360) (MS60, $325-$700)
1918-S obverse (XF40, $55)
1919 reverse (XF40, $70)
1919-D (VF25, $70)
1919-D reverse (MS63, $635)
1919-S (MS62, $515) (MS63, $545)
1919-S obverse (AU58, $285)
1919-S reverse (AU50, $110) (MS61, $520)
1920 obverse (G6, $50) (AU58, $75)
1920-D (VG10, $15) (AU53, $275) (MS60, $1,040)
1920-D obverse (VF25, $55) (XF45, $75)

1920-S (XF40, $110-$125) (AU50, $145-$160) (AU55, $220)
(MS63, $690) (MS64, $1,600)
1921 (AU58, $80)
1921-S (G4, $40) (VG8, $85) (VG10, $100) (F12, $127) (VF20,
$190-$275)
1921-S obverse (MS64, $1,265)
1921-S reverse (XF45, $170) (AU58, $385) (MS63, $1,495)
1921-S reverse and obverse (VF35, $315)
1923-S (MS62, $285)
1924-D obverse (XF40, $60) (XF45, $105)
1924-S (F12, $55) (VF30, $120) (AU55, $1,150)
1924-S obverse (VF20, $130)
1924-S reverse (MS60, $2,530)
1925-D (VF20, $30) (MS62, $410)
1925-S (XF40, $145) (MS63, $1,400)
1926-D (MS63, $330)
1926-S (VF30, $355)
1927-D (MS61, $110-$125) (MS62, $110)
1927-S (XF45, $35) (AU50, $120) (AU55, $175)
1928-D obverse (MS61, $115)
1929 reverse (MS62, $60)
1931-S (MS62, $125) (MS63, $90)
1935 (F15, $30)
1937 (VF20, $10)
1937-S obverse (MS63, $145)
1938-D obverse (MS65, $30)

Buffalo Nickels
Off center
1913 buffalo on mound (AU58, $240) (MS64, $805-$865)
1913-D buffalo on mound (VF20, $895) (VF30, $80)
1915-S (XF45, $505)
1916 (XF45, $300) (AU55, $660) (MS63, $1,090) (MS64, $2,000)
(MS65, $805-$1,450)
1916-D (genuine, $275) (AU55, $345) (MS64, $489)
1916-S (MS62, $585-$1,265) (MS64, $940)

1917 (VF35, $490) (AU55, $560-$1,725) (AU58, $645-$865)
(MS64, $2,990)
1917-S (AU58, $1,765)
1918 (XF40, $410-$1,495) (AU50, $280) (AU53, $2,300) (AU58,
$1,925) (MS64, $725)
1918-D (MS63, $1,205-$3,000) (MS64, $1,725-$1,900)
1918-S (MS64, $8,625)
1918-S 25% (AU58, $940)
1919 (XF45, $345) *(AU55, $547)* (AU58, $1,150) (MS61, $470)
(MS63, $185-$980) (MS64, $830-$1,095) (MS65, $690-$1,410)
1919-D (MS64, $2,125-$2,990)
1919-S (MS60, $660)
1919-x (MS64, $1,035) (MS65, $860)
1920 (F12, $865) (VF25, $460) (XF45, $185-$415) (AU50, $400-
$1,060) (AU58, $305-$740) (MS62, $540-$705) (MS63, $630-
$1,265) (MS64, $745-$805) (MS65, $1,095)
1920-D (XF45, $280) (AU50, $320)
1920-S (MS63, $4,890) (MS64, $1,840)
1920-x (VF45, $440) (XF40, $410-$980) (AU58, $1,380-$1,880)
(MS62, $890) (MS63, $2,070) (MS64, $805-$17,250)
1921 (MS61, $690)
1921-x (MS63, $2,300)
1925 (MS63, $635) (MS64, $575-$865)
1925-D (XF45, $980)
1926-x (MS63, $2,585)
1928 (VF30, $405)
1928-S (AU58, $750)
1929 (XF45, $980) (MS64, $635)
1929-S (AU58, $545-$635)
1929-x 40% (MS64, $2,590)
1934 (XF40, $185) (MS64, $590)
1935 (AU50, $195-$280) (AU58, $300-$560) (MS60, $230-$385)
(MS62, $250-$2,720) (MS63, $470-$550) (MS64, $255-$690)
(MS65, $1,265-$1,380)
1935 20% (MS65, $840) 2022
1935-x (MS62, $1,725) (MS64, $550)

1936 (VF25, $220) (AU50, $120-$185) (AU55, $530) (AU58, $205-$530) (MS60, $135-$500) (MS62, $250-$520) (MS63, $235-$825) (MS64, $220-$765) (MS65, $440)
1936-x (MS62, $545-$805) (MS63, $575-$920)
1937 (VF30, $1845) (AU50, $155) (MS61, $30) (MS62, $320-$420) (MS63, $350-$540) (MS64, $575) (MS65, $860-$1,035) (MS66, $585-$1,175)

Buffalo Nickels
RPMs/Repunched date/Misplaced
1914 4/3 (G4, $235) (VG8, $225-$285) (VG10, $210-$345) (F12, $325-$510) (VF20, $500-$1,320) (VF35, $630) (XF40, $400-$1,380) (XF45, $325-$825) (AU50, $690-$1,000) (AU53, $750-$1,440) (AU55, $900-$3,500) (AU58, $800-$3,565) (MS62, $865-$4,025) (MS63, $1,425-$6,900) (MS64, $1,200-$12,800) (MS65, $18,400-$63,250)
1914 4/3 (AU50, $890) (MS62, $2,520) (MS63, $2,760)
1915-D D/D (VG10, $185-$260) (F12, $65) (XF40, $255-$260) (AU50, $420-$540) (AU58, $630-$1,150) (MS62, $2,230)
1915-S S/S (G6, $65) (F15, $470) (XF40, $255-$260) (AU58, $1,700)
1918 8/7 (VG8, $930-$1,050) (F12, $1,200) (F15, $1,410) (XF40, $5,520) 2022
1918-D 8/7 (G6, $530-$980) (VG8, $700) (F15, $1,680-$1,995) (VF25, $4,600) (VF30, $4,885-$6,615) (XF45, $4,885-$7,475) (AU53, $13,800) (AU55, $8,400) (MS61, $20,700) (MS62, $33,600-$47,000) (MS63, $51,800) (MS64, $49,000-$85,000) (MS65, $138,000)
1927-D D/D (VG10, $40-$180) (F12, $100) (VF20, $145) (XF40, $215-$290)
1927-D D/D/D (G6, $75)
1930-S S/S (XF40, $140-$145) (XF45, $45-$110) (MS62, $430-$435) (MS63, $260) (MS64, $185-$385)
1935-D D/D (VG8, $65-$165) (F12, $75-$90) (XF40, $990-$995) (AU50, $200-$360) (AU53, $190-$290) (AU55, $225-$265) (MS66, $430-$435)

1936-D D/D (XF45, $65) (MS64, ($100-$255) (MS65, $100-$490) (MS66, $125-$540)
1936-S S/S (VF30, $45-$70) (XF45, $20-$90) (AU50 $50) (AU58-$165-$255) (MS62, $155) (MS64, $100-$415) (MS65, $250-$825)
1937-D D/D (MS63, $30-$35) (MS65, $45-$190) (MS66, $85-$155)
1938-D D/D (AU58, $35-$40) (MS63, $22-$70) (MS64, $15-$75) (MS65, $30-$105) (MS66, $50-$185) (MS67, $120-$3,065) 2022
1938-D D/D/S (MS65, $125-$355) (MS66, $325) (MS67, $3,225) (MS68, $3,420) 2022
1938-D D/S (XF40, $35-$40) (AU58, $35-$70) (MS62, $45) (MS63, $45-$90) (MS64, $65-$145) (MS65, $70-$235) (MS66, $95-$230) (MS67, $3,360) (MS68, $3,120) 2022

Buffalo Nickels
Split
1913 (VF30, $140) (AU55, $605) 2022
1913 buffalo on flat ground, obverse (MS63, $20)
1913 buffalo on flat ground, 10% off center, cracked (MS64, $800)
1913 buffalo on raised ground, obverse (AU55, $605)
1914 obverse (VF30, $290) (XF40, $50)
1914-x obverse (VF30, $30)
1916 obverse (F12, $130) (VF30, $75) 2022
1917 obverse (XF40, $200) 2022
1917 reverse (VF20, $80) 2022
1919 obverse (VF30, $470)
1919-x 2.3 grams (MS63, $345)
1919-x (MS63, $345)
1920 before strike (MS64, $775)
1920-D w/ragged clip 6% (AU58, $470) 2022
1920-x obverse (MS64, $325)
No date before strike, obverse (no grade, $345) 2022
No date before strike, obverse, 2.4 grams (no grade, $160-$345)
No date obverse (no grade, $575) (VG8, $60) (VG10, $40-$100)
No date reverse (MS62, $130)

Buffalo Nickels
Striking Errors
1913 buffalo on raised mound, double struck, rotated (MS63, $5,100)
1913-D broadstruck (VF25, $405-$585)
1913-S broadstruck (F15, $200)
1917-S broadstruck (MS64, $1,725)
1918 double struck, w/indent (MS64, $1,725)
1919 broadstruck (AU50, $205) (AU53, $160)
1920 broadstruck (MS66, $1,035)
1920-S double struck (AU55, $8,050)
1924 double struck & rotated (F12, $2,235-$3,675)
1935 double struck & rotated (XF45, $2,300)
1936 broadstruck (MS62, $150-$345)
1936 double struck, w/flipover (MS64, $4,200-$4,600)
1936-S double struck & rotated (VF20, $1,850)

Buffalo Nickels
Variations
1913 buffalo on flat ground (MS64, $105-$200) (MS65, $85-$255) (MS66, $450-$1,650) (MS67, $3,120-$9,400) (PR62, $25,875) (PR63, $94,000) (PR65, $880-$2,500) (PR66, $990-$4,700) (PR67, $2,100-$9,250) (PR68, $5,750-$63,250)
1913 buffalo on mound (XF40, $15) (MS60, $15-$140) (MS62, $25-$780) (MS63, $20-$245) (MS64, $30-$245) (MS65, $40-$230) (MS66, $40-$1,500) (MS67, $155-$4,700) (MS68, $4,700-$22,325) (PR65, $1,160-$4,300) (PR66, $1,560-$6,465) (PR67, $960-$18,400) (PR68, $16,100-$29,900)
1913 3½ legs, buffalo on mound (MS63, $3,700-$4,230) (MS64, $4,900-$12,925) (MS65, $47,450) (MS66, $21,150)
1913-D buffalo on mound (G6, $10) (XF45, $10-$25) (AU55, $240-$245) (MS60, $35-$155) (MS62, $40-$320) (MS63, $35-$175) (MS64, $60-$430) (MS65, $95-$1,295) (MS66, $245-$3,250) (MS67, $1,000-$5,400)

1913-D buffalo on flat ground (VF20, $35-$55) (VF35, $155-$160) (XF, $60-$320) (MS60, $80-$215) (MS63, $145-$485) (MS64, $320-$1,030) (MS65, $400-$2,230) (MS66, $1,600-$5,100) (MS67, $5,465-$23,000)

1913-D two feathers (XF40, $90) (XF45, $125-$130) (AU55, $135-$145) (MS62, $190-$195) (MS63, $100-$180)

1913-S buffalo on flat ground (F12, $170-$180) (VF25, $400-$430) (VF30, $410-$430) (XF45, $195-$530) (MS60, $450-$825) (MS62, $1,550-$1,645) (MS63, $1,520) (MS64, $1,165-$2,225) (MS65, $4,850) (MS66, $2,450-$27,500) (MS67, $2,450-$47,000)

1913-S buffalo on mound (F12, $30) (VF30, $40-$65) (VF35, $40-$45) (XF45, $35-$390) (MS60, $55-$115) (MS62, $90-$350) (MS63, $95-$430) (MS64, $230-$250) (MS65, $175-$4,700) (MS66, $690-$5,520) (MS67, $1,950-$8,800)

1915 two feathers (VG8, $45-$50) (F15, $115-$280) (VF25, $165) (XF40, $355-$380) (XF45, $330) (AU55, $165-$470) (AU58, $650-$675) (MS62, $900) (MS63, $3,055) (MS64, $125-$1,920) (MS67, $3,050-$3,100)

1915-D two feathers (VF30, $255-$260) (XF45, $900)

1916 two feathers (F12, $50) (VF20, $35-$50) (VF25, $55-$65) (XF45, $80-$125) (AU50, $105-$110) (AU53, $175-$180) (AU55, $170-$180) (AU58, $145-$405) (MS61, $95-$100) (MS62, $205-$450) (MS63, $225-$300) (MS64, $180-$400)

1917 two feathers (F12, $40-$45) (VF30, $545) (XF40, $125) (XF45, $50-$590) (AU50, $130) (AU58, $640-$645) (MS60, $180) (MS65, $2,055)

1917-D 3½ legs (G6, $70-$220) (VG8, $70-$635) (VF30, $455) (VF 35, $255) (AU58, $1,725) (MS63, $2,640)

1917-D two feathers (F12, $100-$110)

1917-S two feathers (G6, $20-$105) (VG10, $195-$200) (F12, $200) (F15, $65) (VF25, $175-$305) (VF30, $305-$545) (VF35, $235) (XF40, $260-$330) (XF45, $3,290) (AU50, $325-$355) (AU58, $995-$1,000) (MS64, $2,580) (MS65, $7,920)

1925-S two feathers (VG8, $55) (VG10, $90-$95) (F12, $20-$115) (F15, $60-$65) (VF20, $40-$520) (VF30, $120-$135) (XF40, $150-$500) (AU50, $375-$380) (MS64, $2,880-$4,400)

1926 (MS64, $600)
1926-D 3½ legs (AU55, $900)
1926-D two feathers (VF25, $100-$105) (MS60, $310-$315)
1927-D 3½ legs (VF30, $290) (AU53, $660) 2022
1927-D two feathers (XF40, $400)
1927-S two feathers (AU58, $645-$650)
1928-S two feathers (MS63, $2,040)
1929-S two feathers (VF20, $80-$120) (XF45, $85-$90) (AU50, $80-$165) (AU53, $410) (MS62, $485-$490) (MS64, $635) (MS65, $485-$3,525)
1930-S two feathers (VG8, $45) (VF20, $115-$250) (VF25, $245) (VF35, $210) (XF40, $410) (XF45, $500)
1936-D 3½ legs (G6, $395) (F12, $705-$1,050) (F15, $1,115-$1,840) (VF20, $730-$3,200) (VF25, $1,290-$4,315) (VF30, $1,290-$2,990) (VF35, $1,500-$3,450) (XF40, $280-$4,890) (XF45, $1,035-$5,170) (AU50, $3,290-$3,740) (AU53, $3,760) (AU55, $5,175) (AU58, $1,400) (MS62, $12,650-$14,375)
1937-D 3 legs (F15, $470-$480) (VF20, $490) (VF30, $575) (XF40, $720) (VF20, $600-$650) (VF30, $575-$720) (XF40, $525-$580) (XF45, $750-$780) (AU53, $870) (AU55, $1,000-$1,920) (AU58, $1,080-$1,530) (MS60, $420) (MS62, $2,220-$2,520) (MS63, $4,560-$6,900) (MS64, $5,520-$8,050) (MS65, $14,400-$18,600) (MS66, $26,400-$86,250) 2022

Buffalo Nickels
Wrong US and Foreign Planchets
1913 dime planchet (MS66, $46,000)
1913-S type I planchet (MS64, $920)
1913-S type II planchet (MS64, $865-$1,100)
1918-S silver dime planchet (AU58, $9,250)
1919 one cent planchet (MS61, $4,500)
1920 one cent planchet (XF40, $2,000) (MS64, $12,350)

Jefferson Nickels 1938-date

1938-2004   2005

2006-date

The coin's obverse has changed three times since the first mintage in 1938. The coin's reverse was temporarily changed from 1942 through 1945, adding a large mintmark over the dome, distinguishing the silver issues from the nickel alloy. The coin's reverse was changed in 2004 and 2005, hosting four different designs to celebrate 200 years of the westward expansion with the Louisiana purchase. The obverse of the Jefferson nickel was changed in 2006 with a forward-looking design.

Weight 5 grams
Diameter .835 in
Thickness 1.95 mm

Jefferson Nickels
Blank Planchet
No date (no grade, $85)

No date proof ($90)
No date silver (no grade, $195)

Jefferson Nickels
Canceled
No date (no grade, $70)

Jefferson Nickels
Clip Planchets
1945-P curved, w/cracked planchet (MS65, $35)
1976 curved, w/40% off center (MS66, $65-$70)
1976-D curved (MS60, $75) (MS66, $85)
1980-D double (MS67, $130)
1985-P (MS63, $65)
No date (MS63, $140)
No date double curved (MS64, $140)

Jefferson Nickels
Cracked and Defective
1971 cracked & defective (AU58, $185)
1995-P defective (MS65, $975)
No date defective (MS63, $1060-$1,100)

Jefferson Nickels
Cuds and Retained Cuds
1940-S 10% (VF20, $145)
1943-P 25%/25% (MS63, $520)
1944-P 10% (VF25, $125)
1962-D 10% (XF45, $125)
1967 10% (XF40, $20) (AU55, $40) (AU58, $45)
1967 25% (AU58, $195)
1969-S 10% (MS65, $95) (PR68, $1,265)
1970-D 10% (MS60, $95) (MS64, $160)
1970-D 10%/10%, 2 cuds (MS63, $200)
1972 15% (MS66, $185)

1972-D 10% (MS64, $40-$60) (MS65, $65) (MS66, $55-$210)
(AU55, $160)
1974-D 10% (AU58, $105) (MS65, $115)
1976-S 50% (PR67, $400) (PR68, $175)
1978-D 10% (AU58, $135) (MS65, $40)
1981-P 10% (MS65, $165)
1982-P 10% (AU50, $20) (MS64, $30)
1983-P 10% (AU58, $140) (MS64, $135)
1984-P 10% (MS62, $100)
1989-P 10% (AU50, $20) (MS63, $35)
1994-P 10% reverse (MS60, $75)
1998-P 10% (MS64, $125)
1999-D 15% (MS63, $155)
2006-P 10% reverse (MS64, $20)

Jefferson Nickels
Die Adjustment Strike
1963-D (MS60, $50)
1964-D (MS60, $175)
1970-S (NG, $240-$255) (MS60, $255)
1991-D (MS60, $30)
2004-P Peace Metal (MS60, $435)
No date (NG, $285)
No date (MS60, $300)

Jefferson Nickels
Doubled Dies
1938 DDO (MS64FS, $500)
1938 DDO quadrupled (MS64, $115-$140) (MS66, $200-$400)
1938-D DDR (MS64, $35-$40) (MS66, $25-$30)
1939 DDO (AU58, $125) (MS64, $25) (MS65, $55-$200)
1939 DDO/DDR (MS65, $55-$60)
1939 DDR (XF40, $50) (AU50, $130) (AU58, $80-$85) (MS62,
$410-$415) (MS63, $600) (MS64, $90) (MS65, $60)
1939 doubled Monticello (VF30, $45-$140) (XF40, $55-$120)
(AU50, $120) (AU53, $180) (AU55, $160-$225) (AU58, $160-

$350) (MS60, $265) (MS63, $240) (MS64, $220-$1,050) (MS65, $385-$2,550) (MS65 FS, $11,100) (MS66, $525-$2,400) (MS66 FS, $1,100-$6,900) (MS67, $1,900-$3,100) (MS67 FS, $1,880-$20,560) 2022

1939 DDR, quadrupled (MS64, $165) (MS65, $255-$450) (MS66, $225-$940) (MS67, $1055-$3,055)

1939-S DDO, quadrupled (MS67, $1055)

1939-S DDR (MS64, $25) 2022

1940-D DDR (MS65 $30-$115)

1942 DDO (MS64, $90-$160) (MS65, $375) (MS65 FS, $500) (MS66, $775)

1942 DDO, type I[34] (MS63, $120) (MS65, $690) (MS66 FS, $3,000)

1942 DDR, type I (PR64, $55)

1942-S DDO (MS65, $30-$70)

1943-P DDO (F12, $10) (AU50, $60) (AU58, $75-$185) (MS60, $110) (MS63, $1,680) (MS64, $140-$400) (MS65, $80-$635) (MS65FS, $662-$965) (MS66, $260-$1,550) (MS66FS, $600-$2,350) (MS67, $650-$11,500) 2022

1943-S DDR (MS62, $10)

1945-P DDR (XF40, $40) (MS63, $95-$230) (MS64, $30-$375) (MS64FS, $160) (MS65, $80-$1,450) (MS65FS, $75-$5,200) (MS66, $150-$5,200) (MS66FS, $1,600-$14,100) (MS67, $1,800-$3,800) 2022

1945-S DDR (MS64, $30) (MS65, $40-$80)

1946-S DDO (MS64, $280-$1,050) (MS65, $1,000-$2,875) (MS66, $1,175)

1951 DDO (PR65, $55) (PR66, $80-$150) (PR67, $75-$400) (PR68, $440-$6,450) (PR69, $3,525)

1953 DDO (PR65, $20) (PR66 Cameo, $60-$85) (PR67, $90-$310) (PR67 Cameo, $200-$255) (PR68, $545-$650) (PR68 Cameo, $500-$6,450) (PR69, $630-$4,700)

1954-S DDO (MS65, $125) (MS66, $365) 2022

1954-S DDR (MS64, $60) (MS65, $130-$300)

---

[34] Type I are Jefferson nickels minted with nickel content. Type II Jefferson nickels are minted with silver content.

1955 DDR (PR65, $30-$50) (PR67, $110-$120)
1955 DDR, tripled (PR64, $40) (PR67, $150) (PR68, $200-$330)
1955-D DDR (MS64, $20-$30)
1956 DDO (PR66, $40) (PR67, $75-$155) (PR68, $40-$325)
1956 DDR (F12, $15) (PR67, $30)
1956 DDR, quadrupled (MS64, $140) (MS65, $120-$135) 2022
1956 DDR, tripled (MS65, $160) (MS66, $90) (MS67, $285)
1957 DDO (MS65, $65)
1957 DDO, quadrupled (PR67, $220)
1957 DDR, quadrupled (MS65, $140)
1959 DDR (MS64, $30-$35)
1960 DDO/DDR (PR66, $60-$65)
1960 DDR (PR66, $30-$65) (PR67, $30)
1960 DDR, quadrupled (PR65, $130-$285) (PR66, $365-$380)
(PR67, $650-$1,000)
1960-D DDR (MS64, $30-$35) (MS65, $30)
1961 DDR (MS65 FS, $130) (PR66, $10) (PR67, $25)
1961 DDR, tripled (PR66, $415) (PR67, $425)
1962 DDR (MS65, $40-$45) (PR66, $30-$35)
1963 DDR (PR67, $35-$45)
1964 DDR (PR66, $40) (PR67, $25-$60)
1990-S DDO (PR69, $520-920)
1990-S DDO, w/off center (PR69, $375)
2004-P handshake DDO (MS63, $75) (MS64, $50)
2004-P peace metal DDO (MS64, $50-$100)

Jefferson Nickels
Filled Dies
1979-S filled S (PR70, $155) 2022
1981-S filled S (PR70, $200) 2022

Jefferson Nickels
Fragment
1943 w/strike through reverse (MS63, $155) 2022
1945-P w/strike through (MS63, $285)
1959-D w/strike through (MS65, $75) 2022

2000-D w/multiple strike, thin (MS62, $375-$455) 2022
No date (MS62, $630) (MS64, $85) 2022
Jefferson Nickels
Lamination
1952 (F15, $35)

Jefferson Nickels
Off center
1939 (MS64, $230) (MS65, $185-$220)
1940 (MS64, $220)
1940-S (AU55, $70) (MS66, $550)
1941 (AU58, $130) (MS62, $10) (MS64, $175) (MS65, $235-$375)
1941-S (AU50, $25)
1942-P 40% (MS62, $1,410) (MS64, $1,560)
1943-P (MS64, $50)
1944-P (AU50, $275) (MS63, $80) (MS64FS, $1,060)
1945-P (AU50, $40) (MS65FS, $135-$290)
1945-S AU55, $165)
1948-S (MS64FS, $325-$390)
1949-D D/S (AU55, $460)
1949-S (MS66, $645-$690)
1952-S (MS64, $635)
1953-S (MS65, $545-$550) (MS66, $560-$635)
1954-D (MS66, $110)
1954-S (MS61, $255)
1955-D (MS66, $405)
1957-D (MS67, $370-$460)
1959-D (MS64, $130)
1961 (PR66, $3,450-$4,025)
1961-D (AU58, $345)
1964 (MS62, $60) (MS63, $50) (MS65, $195)
1964-D (MS60, $175) (MS62, $190)
1965 (MS64, $65-$375)
1968-D 68% (MS67, $150)
1968-S (MS63, $60)

1970-D (MS62, $180) (MS63, $20-$25) (MS64, $160) (MS66, $105)
1970-S (MS62, $20-$95) (MS63, $35)
1971-D (AU58, $330) (MS64, $100)
1972-D (MS60, $20) (MS63, $25-$210) (MS65, $30)
1974 (MS66, $190)
1975-D (MS64, $45) (MS65, $50)
1976 (MS63, $100-$765) (MS64, $60-$105) (MS67, $210)
1976-D (MS63, $85) (MS64, $60) (MS66, $65-$85)
1977 (MS65, $15)
1978 (MS62, $30) (MS64, $40-$65)
1979 (MS60, $130) (MS65, $30)
1980-D (MS64, $1,265) (MS67, $1,495)
1980-P (MS60, $25) (MS64, $45-$140)
1981-P (MS64, $140)
1983-D (MS66, $160)
1984-P (MS62, $20)
1985-D (MS60, $30) (MS66, $160)
1985-P (MS60, $20)
1986-D (MS62, $55)
1987-P (MS64, $140)
1987-D (MS63, $35)
1989-P 55% (MS60, $45) (MS62, $25-$40)
1993-D (MS63, $10)
1994-P (MS64, $20-$40) (MS65, $50)
1995-P (MS60, $35-$85) (MS64, $55-$65)
1996-P (MS60, $20-$45) (MS64, $30-$230) (MS65, $40) (MS65, $40-$130)
1998-P (MS64, $10)
1999-P (MS65, $15-$130) (MS66, $15-$65)
1999-D (MS63, $25-$35) (MS64, $20-120) (MS65, $20-$50) (MS66, $40-$80) (MS67, $110)
2000-D (MS63, $55) (MS64, $45-$95) (MS65, $20-$40) (MS66, $25-$50) (MS67, $140)
2005-P (MS63, $130)
2006-P (MS66FS, $435)

2011-P (AU50, $75)

Jefferson Nickels
RPMs/Repunched date/Misplaced
1938-D D/D (MS62, $30) (MS65, $125) (MS66, $52)
1938-D/S (MS65, $145) (MS66, $120-$360) (MS67, $525-$1,495)
1940-S S/S (MS64, $25) (MS65, $30-$210) (MS65 FS, $350)
(MS66, $130-$355) 2022
1941-D D/D (MS65, $1,115-$1,125)
1941-S S/S (MS66, $1,175)
1942-D D over horizontal D (F12, $45-$55) (VF20, $65-$95)
(XF45, $70-$525) (AU50, $230) (AU55, $275-$1,645) (MS60,
$1,600) (MS63, $3,000-$4,400) (MS63FS, $8,050) (MS64,
$1,250-$8,625) (MS64FS, $5,400-$32,200) (MS65, $4,400-
$14,950) (MS65FS, $1,265-$30,550) (MS66, $3,500-$17,000)
(MS66FS, $1,200-$31,725)
1942-S S/S (MS63, $95) (MS64, $115)
1943-D D/D (MS64, $85) (MS65, $25-$85) (MS66, $30-$265)
1943-D D/D/D (MS64, $30) (MS65, $35) (MS66, $50-$90)
1943-P 3/2 (AU55, $200-$250) (AU58, $200-$225) (MS63, $200-
$370) (MS64, $200-$840) (MS64FS, $300-$800) (MS65, $330-
$1,100) (MS65FS, $760-$2,000) (MS66, $500-$3,800) (MS66FS,
$2,100-$2,300) (MS67, $1,450-$4,200) (MS67FS, $2,530-
$16,675) (MS68, $3,400-$4,300) 2022
1943-P 3/2, DDO (MS64, $190) (MS66FS, $1,000-$2,600)
(MS67, $5,600-$6,500) 2022
1944-D D/D (MS64, $25-$65) (MS66, $75-$310)
1945-D D/D (MS63, $15) (MS65, $25-$35) (MS66, $20) (MS67,
$75-$80)
1945-P/P/P (MS65, $225-$950) (MS65FS, $1,300) (MS66, $1175-
$2600) (MS67, $1,300)
1945-P/P/P, DDR (MS66, $1,495)
1946-D D over inverted D (AU50, $100) (MS64, $630) (MS65,
$720-$940) (MS66, $1,320) (MS66FS, $1,235-$1,525) (MS67,
$1,300) 2022

1946-D D over horizontal D (AU55, $165) (MS60, $205-$210)
(MS64, $1,350-$2,000) (MS65, $1,495) (MS65FS, $1,250-$1,400)
(MS66, $1,350-$5,600) (MS66FS, $2,100-$3,700)
1946-D D/D (VF30, $30) (MS64, $1,265-$3,220) (MS65, $1,725-
$3,000) (MS66FS, $1,650-$11,500)
1948-D D/D (MS65, $35)
1949-D D/S (MS64, $165-$650) (MS65, $280-$8,050) (MS66,
$480-$1,880) (MS66FS, $920-$8,050) (MS67, $800-$2,600)
(MS67FS, $32,900)
1951-S S/S (MS65, $80)
1953-D D over inverted D (MS63, $125-$140) (MS64, $90-$225)
(MS65, $250-$260) 2022
1954-D D/D (MS60, $10)
1954-S S/D (MS64, $35-$250) (MS65, $50-$575) (MS66, $330-
$3,450)
1954-S/S (MS65, $115) 2022
1955-D D/D (MS64, $30)
1955-D D/D/D (MS64, $40)
1955-D D/S (MS63, $40-$65) (MS64, $30-$1,500) (MS65, $50-
$475) (MS66, $170-$3,740) 2022
1968-S S/S (PR67, $400)
1964-D D/D (MS65, $1,750-$2,800)
1975-D misplaced mintmark (none at auction) 2022
1999-D D/S (MS66, $375)

Jefferson Nickels
Split
1941-S before strike, obverse, 3.3 grams (no grade, $80)
1942-P (VG8, $10)
1942 (AU50, $40)
1942-S (MS65, $20)
1943-P (AU50, $15) (MS63, $210)
1943-P obverse (AU55, $65) 2022
1944-D (MS65, $25)
1944-P (F12, $15) (VF20, $20-$25) (VF25, $10) (XF40, $10)
1944-P before strike, obverse (no grade, $165)

1944-P obverse, w/clamshell (VF25, $100) 2022
1944-P obverse (MS64, $260)
1945-P (MS63, $50) (MS64, $15) (MS65, $10-$15)
1945-P obverse (VF35, 130)
1946 obverse (no grade, $40)
1946 reverse (AU55, $104) 2022
1947 (MS62, $160)
1947 obverse (MS62, $40)
1949 obverse (V20, $115)
1952 (XF40, $325) 2022
1953 obverse (VF30, $385)
1953-D before strike, obverse (no grade, $125)
1955-D before strike, obverse, 3.5 grams (no grade, $25)
1956-D obverse, 2.5 grams (no grade, $145) 2022
1957 obverse (no grade, $130)
1958-D before strike, obverse (MS63, $120)
1959 after stike, obverse (AU58, $45)
1960 before strike, obverse, 2.5 grams (no grade, $65)
1960 obverse (AU58, $50)
1960-D broadstruck, obverse (no grade, $130) (MS64, $45)
1960-D obverse (MS62, $100)
1961-D before strike, obverse (MS62, $80)
1962-D (AU55, $45)
1964-D (AU58, $10)
1964-D obverse (MS60, $50)
1964-D obverse, 3.1 grams (no grade, $60) 2022
1966 (MS65, $110)
1973-D before strike, obverse, 3.4 grams (genuine, $85) 2022
1974-D before strike, obverse, 2.56 grams (genuine, $210)
1976-D before strike, obverse, 3.4 grams (genuine, $85)
No date war nickel (F12, $10) (MS60, $200)
No date after strike, obverse (AU53, $65) 2022
No date obverse, 2.4 grams, w/off center (genuine, $210)
No date reverse (MS66, $60) 2022
No date reverse, 3.7 grams (MS62, $120) 2022
No date war nickel, reverse (MS63, $50) 2022

Jefferson Nickels
Striking Errors
1938 broadstruck, w/partial brockage (MS65, $55)
1939 quadrupled reverse (MS64, $165) (MS65, $255-$450)
(MS66, $225-$940) (MS67, $1055-$3,055)
1941 mated pair (MS65, $2,760)
1945-P broadstruck (MS62, $805)
1951 double struck, w/80% off center (MS63, $145)
1952 brockage, obverse (AU55, $150)
1952 double struck (AU58, $300) (MS62, $195) (MS64, $440)
1964 broadstruck, w/brockage (MS64, $55-$65) (MS66, $165)
(MS67, $285)
1964 broadstrike, w/brockage (MS63, $405)
1964 double struck (MS63, $210) (MS63, $270) (MS64, $345)
1964 mated pair (PR66, $5,170)
1964 mated pair, w/double strike (MS65, $3,000) 2022
1964 triple struck (MS65, $500)
1964-D double struck (MS62, $75)
1966 double struck (MS62, $660) (MS65, $375)
1967 double struck (MS64, $320)
1968-D triple struck (MS64, $1,150)
1968-S capped die, w/strike through (MS65, $90) 2022
1968-S double struck & rotated (PR63, $2,235)
1970-D double struck (AU58, $250-$345) (MS62, $200) (MS64,
$250-$865) (MS66, $255)
1970-S broadstruck, w/double strike & strike through (MS67,
$2,100)
1970-x double struck (MS63, $135)
1971-D double struck (MS62, $410) (MS64, $300)
1972-D counter brockage (MS64, $520)
1972-S double struck (PR67, $4,315)
1973 double struck, w/75% off center (MS60, $60)
1973-D chain struck, w/60% off center & counting wheel damage
(MS60, $385) (MS62, $1,020) 2022
1974-D double struck (MS60, $40)

1976-D double struck (MS60, $235-290) 2022
1977 double struck (MS60, $25-$105)
1977-D broadstruck (MS66, $90)
1977-D brockage, w/obverse die cap (MS66, $3,220)
1977-D multiple struck (MS68, $950)
1977-S double struck, w/off center (PR66, $1,080)
1979-D double struck, w/65% off center (MS65, $805)
1980-D double struck (MS62, $80) (MS63, $40)
1980-P double struck (MS60, $20-$190) (MS64, $460)
1980-P mated pair (MS66, $7,500)
1980-P obverse brockage (MS63, $100)
1980-P triple struck (MS63, $520)
1981-D double struck, w/85% off center (MS60, $20)
1981-P bonded pair (MS65, $1,610) (MS66, $1,500)
1981-P double struck (MS60, $15-$165) (MS65, $115)
1981-P partial brockage (MS64, $1,100)
1982-P double struck, w/off center (AU55, $40) 2022
1983-P brockage, w/40% off center (MS64, $55)
1983-P broadstruck, w/brockage (AU55, $15)
1983-P double struck, w/5% off center (MS60, $25-$50) (MS61, $50) (MS62, $35) (MS63, $35-$105) (MS64, $35-$130) (MS65, $35-$50)
1983-P brockage, w/partial colar (MS64, $125)
1984-P double struck (MS62, $90) (MS64, $80) (MS65, $320)
1984-P double struck, w/75% off center (MS60, $35)
1985-P double struck (AU55, $55) (MS62, $95) (MS64, $115)
1986-P double struck (MS63, $80)
1988-D multiple struck, w/60% off center (MS67, $105)
1989-P triple struck (MS64, $405)
1990-P brockage, w/double strike (MS64, $220)
1990-P brockage, obverse, w/double struck (MS64, $220)
1993-P double struck (MS61, $55-$75) (MS65, $85)
1995-P bonded, w/double strike (MS63, $1,950)
1995-P brockage, w/10% off center (MS64, $20)
1995-P broadstruck, w/brockage (MS64, $20)
1995-P brockage, w/partial collar (MS64, $45)

1995-P double struck (MS60, $60) (MS63, $50) (MS64, $105) (MS65, $20) (MS66, $750)
1996-D double struck (MS65, $105)
1996-D saddle struck (MS64, $45)
1996-P double struck (MS63, $285)
1996-P triple struck (MS64, $230)
1998-D double struck (MS63, $40)
1998-P broadstruck, w/brockage (MS65, $95)
1998-P double struck (MS63, $325)
1998-P double struck, w/flip over (MS64, $605)
1998-P multiple struck (MS63, $550)
1998-P triple struck (MS60, $250) (MS64, $1,645)
1999-D die cap, obverse (MS64, $1,050)
1999-D double struck (AU58, $25) (MS 61, $55) (MS63, $45-$150) (MS64, $21-$110) (MS65, $85)
1999-P bonded, w/multiple strikes (MS67, $2,650)
1999-P broadstruck (MS66, $160)
1999-P broadstruck, w/indent (MS66, $85-$90) 2022
1999-P brockage (MS64, $25-$85) (MS65, $185)
1999-P broadstruck, w/brockage (MS66, $115-$180)
1999-P brockage, w/partial collar (MS64, $85)
1999-P quadruple struck, w/die clash (MS65, $450)
1999-P chain struck, w/indent & triple struck (MS62, $565) 2022
1999-P double struck (MS64, $185-$215)
1999-P feeder finger (MS65, $3,000)
1999-P mated pair (MS65, $300)
No date broadstruck (XF45, $150)
No date broadstruck, w/brockage (MS60, $55) (MS64, $40-$125) (MS65, $105-$635) (MS66, $60-$210) (MS67, $90)
No date brockage (XF45, $150) (MS62, $45) (MS63, $30-$280) (MS65, $200)
No date brockage, w/multiple strike (MS66FS, $115)
No date brockage, w/partial collar (MS64, $30)
No date capped die (MS63, $240)
No date counter brockage (MS63, $430)
No date die cap reverse, w/double strikes (MS64, $85)

No date die cap, w/strike through (MS64, $460)
No date multiple struck (MS64, $130)
No date double struck (MS60, $30) (MS63, $20-$565) (MS64, $75-$820) (PR65, $3,960)
No date brockage, w/double strikes (MS63, $90) (MS65, $90) (MS68, $220)
No date double struck, w/flip over (MS63, $210) (PR64, $105)
No date double struck, w/saddle struck (MS63, $105-$345) (MS65, $245)
No date double struck, w/saddle strike & curved clip (MS66, $690)
No date double struck, w/saddle strike & straight clip (MS66, $435)
No date brockage, w/multiple strikes (MS66, $150)
No date quadruple struck (MS62, $795)
No date saddle struck, w/triple strikes (MS67, $920)
No date triple struck (MS62, $165)

Jefferson Nickels
Thin
1960-D thin (MS60, $25)

Jefferson Nickels
Wrong US and Foreign Planchets
1941 Lincoln cent planchet (VF20, $940) (AU58, $940) (MS63, $780)
1942 silver planchet (G6, $9,987)
1943 steel cent planchet (AU55, $1,800-$3,750)
1943-D Australian sixpence planchet (AU58, $1,055)
1943-D copper planchet (MS64, $1,680-$1,850)
1943-S steel one cent planchet (AU55, $4,110)
1944-D dime planchet (AU58, $1,740)
1944-P bronze one cent planchet (MS64, $3,500)
1944-P copper-nickel planchet (VF30, $6,900)
1945-P one cent planchet (MS64, $3,290)
1945-S dime planchet (AU58, $1,680)
1952 dime planchet (AU55, $430)

1955 dime planchet (AU55, $500-$1,035)

1957 one cent planchet (MS60, $340) (MS63, $340-$360)

1958 one cent planchet (MS63, $520)

1958 silver dime planchet (AU58, $660) (MS65, $645)

1961 one cent planchet (MS64, $350)

1961-D dime planchet (MS60, $750)

1962 one cent planchet (MS63, $350)

1962-D one cent planchet (MS64, $930)

1963 one cent planchet (MS61, $385)

1964 one cent planchet (MS63, $470-$520)

1964-D one cent planchet (MS62, $360) (MS64, $360-$4,300)

1965 dime planchet (MS65, $535)

1966 dime planchet (MS65, $380)

1968-S one cent planchet (MS64, $485) (MS65, $630)

1970 dime planchet (MS62, $315)

1970-S one cent planchet (MS63, $580)

1971 dime planchet (MS63, $600)

1972-D one cent planchet (VF20, $80) (MS64, $360-$660)

1974 one cent planchet (MS64, $660)

1974-D one cent planchet (MS66, $580)

1976 dime planchet (MS64, $520)

1976 Philippine 1S planchet (MS62, $825)

1976-D one cent planchet (MS61, $240) (MS62, $275) (MS63, $195)

1976-D one cent planchet (AU58, $200)

1976-D one cent planchet, off center (MS64, $2,700)

1976-S one cent planchet (PR63, $2,640)

1977 1976 one cent (MS64, $4,600)

1977 1977 one cent (MS66, $990)

1977 dime planchet (MS63, $315) (MS64, $1,840)

1977 dime planchet, obverse dent (MS66, $555-$560)

1977-D one cent planchet (XF45, $70)

1977-S one cent planchet (PR64, $2,800) PR66, $1,560)

1977-S dime planchet (MS68, $9,300) (PR67, $1,500-$3,120) (PR68, $4,200)

1977-S dime planchet, w/die clash (PR67, $1,620)

1978 one cent planchet (AU55, $220) (MS60, $195-$245) (MS64, $220)

1979 one cent planchet (MS62, $205) (MS64, $220) (MS65, $975-$1,500)

1979-D one cent planchet (MS64, $135)

1980-P one cent planchet (MS63, $520-$1,840) (MS64, $880-$2,750) (MS65, $1,005)

1980-P one cent planchet (MS63, $355-$415) (MS64, $260)

1980-D one cent planchet (MS65, $345)

1981-P one cent planchet (MS63, $600) (MS64, $1,095)

1982-D one cent planchet (MS63, $240) (MS64, $375)

1984-P one cent planchet (MS62, $530)

1984-P dime planchet, w/broadstrike (MS67, $585-$1,065)

1984-P dime planchet, w/double strike (MS64, $1,495)

1985-D one cent planchet (MS64, $810)

1986-P one cent planchet (MS60, $325)

1989-P one cent planchet (MS63, $350)

1989-D one cent planchet (MS64, $1,600)

1992-P one cent planchet (MS63, $630)

No date one cent planchet (MS60, $245) (MS63, $245) (MS64, $750-$980)

1998-P one cent planchet (MS67, $1,020)

1998-P dime planchet (MS65, $385) 2022

1999-P one cent planchet (MS64, $320)

2000-D one cent planchet (AU50, $435)

2000-P one cent planchet (MS65, $1,110)

2000-P 1978 cent (MS65, $2,880)

No date clad dime planchet (MS64, $185)

No date clad dime planchet (MS64, $1,880)

No date silver dime planchet (MS62, $635-$690) (MS63, $1,150-$1,450)

No date dime planchet (AU58, $425) (MS64, $205)

No date dime planchet (MS64, $820-$955)

No date nickel planchet type I (MS63, $1,265)

No date one cent planchet (MS64, $155)

No date one cent planchet, w/doubled struck & saddle struck

Jefferson Nickels
Variations
1938 re-engraved obverse (PR65, $100) (PR66, $200) 2022
1939 reverse of 1938 (MS63, $10-$60) (MS64, $15-$55) (MS65, $10-$125) (MS66, $15-$65) (MS67, $35-$500) (MS67FS, $1,645) (PR65, $85-$190) (PR66, $115-$170) (PR67, $300-$380) (PR68, $2,990-$11,000) 2022
1939 reverse of 1938, DDR (AU58, $65) (MS60, $120) (PR65, $110)
1939 reverse of 1940 (MS67, $105-$300) (PR66 Cameo, $2,875-$8,625) (PR66, $400-$525) (PR67FS, $900-$3,000) 2022
1939 reverse of 1940, DDR, quadrupled (MS64, $165)
1939-D reverse of 1938 (MS63, $30-$60) (MS64, $35-$65) (MS65, $40-$85) (MS65 FS, $285) (MS66, $50-$500) (MS66 FS, $690-$7,425) (MS67, $65-$2,235) (MS67 FS, $1,100-$3,500) (PR68, $12,925) 2022
1939-D reverse of 1938, DDO (MS67, $175-$500) (MS67 FS, $620-$910)
1939-D reverse of 1940 (MS64, $80) (MS66, $75-$110) (MS66 FS, $565-$3,595) (MS67, $205-$7,475) (MS67 FS, $2,500-$3,120) 2022
1939-S reverse of 1938 (MS64, $165) (MS65, $20-$50) (MS65 FS, $250-$525) (MS66, $40-$250) (MS66 FS, $350-$8,050) (MS67, $200-$1,500)
1939-S reverse of 1940 (MS65, $80) (MS65 FS, $515) (MS66 FS, $2,875) (MS67, $7,800) 2022
1940 reverse of 1938 (PR62, $30-$65) (PR63, $85-$115) (PR64, $120-$400) (PR65, $210-$445) (PR66 Cameo, $8,625) (PR66, $395-$1,325) (PR67, $820-$3,055) (PR68, $1,600-$28,750) 2022
1941-S inverted mintmark (AU58, $75) (MS64, $155) 2022
1941-S large S (MS65, $75-$160) (MS65 FS, $330)
1952 re-engraved obverse (PR66, $110) (PR67, $205)
1954 re-engraved obverse (PR66, $205-$230)
1971 proof, missing S (PR68, $900-$930) (PR69, $2,550-$4,485) 2022

1979-S clear S (PR70, $250) 2022
1981-S clear S (PR70, $750) 2022
2005-D detached leg (MS64, $20-$195) (MS65, $20-$30) (MS66, $35-$40) 2022
2005-D detached leg, speared (MS65, $110) 2022
2005-D speared (MS64, $26-$220) (MS65, $220-$865) (MS66, $765-$1,265) 2022

Chapter Five – Dime Errors 1914-Date

The most revered and widely collected U.S. dime is the Mercury dime. The naming of this dime is incorrect since there was no intention by the mint to associate the obverse with the Roman god Mercury. This coin's more appropriate name could have been winged liberty head since it was the designer's intention. The reverse design shows an ax with wooden spindles tied together.

1935 Mercury dime

Mercury Dimes
Doubled Dies
1928-S DDO (MS65, $1,265-$2,100)
1929-S DDO (MS67, $950-$1,400)
1931-D DDO (AU55, $70)
1931-D DDO/DDR (MS67FB, $2,150)
1931-S DDO (MS62, $115) (MS66FB, $3,750)
1936 DDO (MS62, $65)
1937 DDO (MS64FB, $40)
1937-S DDO (MS68, $470)
1940-S DDO (MS65, $50)
1940-S DDO/DDR (MS65, $660) 2022

Mercury Dimes
Lamination
1921-D (VG8, $75)

1923-S (XF40, $50)
1942 (VF20, $50) (VF35, $15)
1943 w/defective planchet (MS60, $90)

Mercury Dimes
Off center
1916-S (XF45, $55-$210) (MS60, $280)
1917 (AU53, $150) (AU58, $405) (MS63, $220) (MS64, $460-$490)
1917-S (AU58, $320)
1918-D 35% (AU58, $865)
1919 (AU53, $205) (AU58, $220) (MS62, $305)
1919-D (AU55, $220) (MS63, $750)
1920 (MS63, $2,990) (MS64, $460)
1920-D (AU55, $240) (MS62, $370-$1,000) (MS63, $675) (MS64, $940-$1,115)
1920-S (MS62, $920)
1921 (AU55, $865)
1928-S (MS62, $430-$540) (MS63, $405) (MS64, $635-$720) (MS65, $545-$980)
1929-S (AU55, $275) (AU58, $255) (MS60, $115) (MS62FB, $490)
1934-D (AU55, $230) (MS60, $175)
1935 (MS63, $460)
1936 (VF30, $150) (MS61, $345)
1940 (AU58, $80) (MS60, $130) (MS61, $210)
1941 (AU55, $1,265) (MS61, $140) (MS62, $940) (MS63, $405) (MS66, $280)
1941-S (AU58, $110-$140) (MS62, $75-$90) (MS64, $120)
1942 (MS60, $50) (MS62, $490)
1942-D (MS62, $180-$490)
1942-S (MS60, $1,090) (MS63, $195)
1943 (MS62, $140) (MS63, $160)
1943-S (XF40, $100-$140) (AU50, $135) (MS60, $45) (MS62, $195) (MS63, $210)

1944 (AU55, $185) (AU58, $60-$100) (MS61, $460) (MS62, $175) (MS63, $805) (MS64, $170-$1,115) (MS65, $100-$405) (MS65FB, $420)
1944-D (AU58, $220) (MS62, $135)
1944-S (MS60, $105)
1945 (VF30, $80) (AU55, $130) (MS60, $115-$215)
1945-D (MS62, $255)
1945-S (AU50, $40) (MS63, $115)
1945-x (MS63, $460) (MS66, $1,495)
1945-S micro s (AU58, $230) (MS66, $135) 2022

Mercury Dimes
Clipped
1919 straight (MS60, $40)
1921 (F15, $155)
1924 curved (MS66, $305)
1924-D double (MS63, $335)
1928-D curved (MS63, $250)
1934-D curved (MS63, $105)
1936-S curved (MS63, $130)
1941 double (AU50, $25)
1941-D (MS64, $80)
1942 curved (AU58, $25)
1943 ragged (AU50, $90)
1943-S straight (MS65, $70)
1944 curved (AU55, $55) (AU58, $20)
1945-D (AU55, $95)

Mercury Dimes
Inverted Mintmark
1942-S inverted mintmark (MS63, $960) 202

Mercury Dimes
Rotated
1920-D rotated (G6, $35)

Mercury Dimes
RPMs/Repunched date/Misplaced
1916-D D/D (XF40, $3,500)
1934-D D/D (AU55, $65)
1935-S S/S (AU55, $45-$50)
1938-D D/D (MS63, $30-$35)
1939-D D/D (M S65, $75-$80)
1940-D D/D (MS65FB, $185)
1940-S S/S (MS63, $45-$50) (MS65, $55-$110) (MS66, $70-$165) (MS67, $130)
1941-S S/S (AU50, $15) (MS63, $25) (MS64, $35-$190) (MS65, $110-$115) (MS66, $210-$305) (MS66FB, $150-$500)
1942 2/1 (F15-$335) (VF20, $410) (VF25, $375-$435) (VF30, $175-$925) (VF35, $405-$490) (XF40, $510-$555) (XF45, $320-$1,250) (AU50, $750-$840) (AU55, $825-$3,700) (AU58, $1,050-$2,100) (MS60, $2,100-$2,300) (MS62, $1,600-$3,700) (MS63, $2,300-$5,400) (MS63FB, $5,500-$12,000) (MS64, $5,750-$13,500) (MS64FB, $8,000-$9,775) (MS65, $9,775-$20,000) (MS65 FB, $15,000-$25,850) (MS66, $12,000) (MS66FB, $13,500-$76,350) 2022
1942-D 2/1 (G4, $300) (G6, $275) (VG10, $250-$350) (F12, $275-$475) (F15, $275-$400) (VF30, $290) (VF35, $375-$850) (XF40, $575) (XF45, $550-$1,250) (AU50, $670) (AU53, $930) (AU55, $975-$2,000) (AU58, $900-$2,000) (MS60, $850-$4,300) (MS62, $3,000-$5,175) (MS63, $3,800-$7,400) (MS64, $3,800-$7,600) (MS65, $6,900) 2022
1942-D D/D (AU58, $40-$45) (MS64, $45) 2022
1943-S S/S (MS62, $10-$65) (MS65, $250-$260) (MS65FB, $445-$450) (MS67, $1,440-$2,800) 2022
1943-S S/S, w/broadstruck (MS63, $345)
1944-D D/D (MS65, $35-$100) (MS66, $85-$130) (MS67, $275-$355)

Mercury Dimes
Split
1921-D obverse (AU50, $235)

Mercury Dimes
Striking Errors
1914-D partial collar (MS60, $300)
1916 broadstruck (AU58, $230)
1916 partial collar (MS64, $365)
1916 partial collar & tilted (MS64, $325-$350)
1916-S broadstruck (AU50, $345) (AU55, $160)
1917 broadstruck (AU55, $200) (AU58, $180) (MS61, $175)
(MS62, $150) (MS63, $120-$700)
1917 broadstruck, double blank (MS60, $230)
1917-D broadstruck (AU55, $90) (MS63, $420) (MS64, $310-
$415) (MS65, $1,235)
1917-D strike through (AU53, $70)
1917-S broadstruck (XF45, $360)
1918 brockage (MS62, $4,890)
1919 broadstruck (AU50, $100) (MS62, $465) (MS64, $200-$415)
1920 broadstruck (MS60, $90)
1920-D broadstruck (MS60, $150)
1920-S broadstruck (AU55, $200)
1920-S strike through (AU58, $60)
1921 broadstruck (AU55, $1,000)
1924-S broadstruck (MS64, $840)
1924-S strike through, obverse (MS60, $355)
1925 broadstruck (AU55, $110)
1929-D broadstruck (AU55, $115-$200) (MS60, $125) (MS64,
$300-$350)
1929-S broadstruck (AU58, $80)
1934-D broadstruck (MS60, $85-$150) (MS62, $105)
1935 broadstruck (MS64, $205)
1936 broadstruck (AU50, $60)
1937 strike through (MS64, $30)
1938-D strike through (MS66, $50)
1940-S partial collar (MS60, $25)
1941 partial collar & tilted (AU58, $50) (MS60, $70)
1941 broadstruck (MS63, $80) (MS64, $115) (MS66, $165)

1941 double struck (AU58, $1,410)
1941 strike through (MS62, $75)
1941-S broadstruck (AU50, $65) (AU58, $80) (MS63, $195)
(MS64, $140)
1941-S partial collar (MS60, $25) (MS63, $50-$90) (MS64, $60-
$100) (MS66, $70-$80)
1942 broadstruck (MS62, $80) (MS66, $140)
1942-S broadstruck (AU55, $70) (AU58, $90)
1942-S broadstruck, w/strike through (MS63, $200)
1943-S broadstruck (AU50, $115) (MS64, $120)
1944 broadstruck (AU58, $55) (MS60, $50) (MS62, $65-$70)
(MS63, $90-$155) (MS64, $80-$110) (MS65, $130)
1944 partial collar (MS65, $70-$105)
1944 strike through (VF35, $105)
1944-S partial collar (MS66, $135)
1945 broadstruck (AU50, $195) (AU58, $150) (MS60, $55-$140)
(MS63, $165) (MS64, $80-$205) (MS65, $125-$1,120) (MS65FB,
$4,560)
1945 partial collar (XF45, $90) (MS64, $65-$95)
1945 partial collar, tilted (MS65, $645)
1945-D broadstruck (AU58, $45) (MS64, $130)
1945-S broadstruck (AU58, $60)
no date "D," double struck (XF45, $6,040)
no date broadstruck (MS63, $195)

Mercury Dimes
Tapered, Thin and Thick
1945-D tapered (MS64, $45)

Mercury Dimes
Variations
1945-S micro S (MS63, $25) (MS64, $25-$65) (MS65, $45-$845)
(MS65FB, $500-$1,300) (MS66, $115-$240) (MS66FB, $150-
$8,050) (MS67, $265-$7,600) (MS68, $900) (MS68FB, $14,950)
2022

Mercury Dimes
Wrong U.S. and Foreign Planchets
1920 Argentina planchet (F15, $575) (AU55, $500)
1941 Netherlands planchet (MS63, $3,055) (MS64, $2,640)
1942 Ecuador planchet (MS65, $14,375)

Roosevelt Dimes 1946-Date

Weight 2.268 grams
Diameter .705 in
Thickness 1.35 mm

The Roosevelt Dime mintage began in 1946, replacing the
Mercury dime. Until 1965, all Roosevelt dimes were 90 percent
silver and 10 percent copper.

The Roosevelt dime is the only circulating coin to escape major
design modifications by the mint. Even when most U.S. coinage
designs changed in 1976 to display 1776-1976, the dime remained
unchanged. The only change to the Roosevelt dime over its history
is adding the "P" to the coin in 1980.

Roosevelt Dimes
Clad Layer Missing/Improperly Annealed
1970-D no clad layer (MS60, $35)
1974-D improperly annealed (MS64, $65)
1980-P missing clad layer (AU55, $50)

Roosevelt Dimes

Clipped

1946 elliptical (MS64, $50)
1954 curved (MS64, $20)
1956 double (XF45, $15)
1957 curved (AU55, $10)
1960 ragged (AU50, $30)
1963 curved (MS63, $20)
1963 double (XF45, $10-$25)
1963-D curved (AU50, $10)
1964 triple (AU58, $35)
1964-D curved (AU55, $45)
1964-D ragged (AU58, $100) (MS64, $175)
1967 elliptical (MS63, $100)
1967 double (MS63, $60)
1967 elliptical (MS65, $30-$35)
1967 straight (AU50, $35)
196x-x elliptical (MS63, $100)
1975 double ($35)
1976 triple (AU58, $50)
1996-P curved, 10% (MS64, $110)
1998-P curved (MS63, $65)
1998-P double (MS66, $25)
1999-P double, 20%/25% (MS64, $15) (MS66, $20-$65)
1999-P double curved (MS65, $20-$40)
1999-P elliptical (MS64, $65)
2000-P elliptical (MS64, $160)
2001-P triple (MS64, $75-$100)
2002-D straight (MS67, $175)
2003 elliptical (MS66, $175)
2005-P straight, w/off center (MS63, $130)
No date curved (NG, $55)
No date curved, w/off center (MS64, $40)
No date elliptical (MS62, $30-$120)
No date ragged (MS61, $105) (MS62, $50)
No date straight (NG, $45) (MS62, $55)

Roosevelt Dimes
Cuds and Retained Cuds
No date 10% (MS65, $130)
No date 50% (MS63, $920)

Roosevelt Dimes
Die Adjustment Strike
1965 (MS60, $190)
1967 (AU55, $165)
196x (MS60, $125)
1974-D (MS60, $50)
1999-D (MS60, $170)
No date (MS60, $30-$90)
No date (NG, $90)
No date silver (MS60, $110-$245)

Roosevelt Dimes
Die Break
1972-D obverse (MS64, $220)

Roosevelt Dimes
Doubled Dies
1946 DDO (MS64, $30-$45) (MS65, $40-$135) (MS67, $75)
1946 DDO/DDR (MS62, $30-$35) (MS65, $40-$45) (MS67, $70-$75)
1946 DDR (MS65, $40)
1946-D DDO (MS64, $5-$10) (MS66FB, $35-$40)
1946-D DDR (MS63, $30-$35)
1946-S DDO (MS64, $20) (MS66, $25)
1946-S DDR (MS64, $35-$45) (MS65, $70) (MS66, $80-$140) (MS67, $280)
1947-D DDO (MS65, $60)
1947-S DDO (MS64, $10-$40) (MS65, $65)
1947-S DDR (MS64, $40-$100) (MS65, $95) (MS67, $140-$375)
1948 DDO (MS65, $235)
1948 DDR (MS65, $225)

1950 DDR (PR66, $300-$500)
1950-D DDR, die 1 (MS64, $20-$55)
1954 DDO (PR65, $55) (PR66, $45-$100) (PR67, $100-$205)
(PR69, $840) 2022
1954 DDR (MS65, $80) (MS66, $350-$400) (MS67, $100)
1956 DDO (PR64, $30) (PR66, $95) 2022
1956 DDR (PR64, $60)
1960 DDO (PR64, $80-$120) (PR65FB $30-$275) (PR65, $40-
$230) (PR66, $65-$300) (PR67DCAM, $345-$530) (PR67, $105-
$290) (PR68, $60-$995) (PR69, $1,920) 2022
1960 DDR (MS64, $30) (PR64, $30-$55) (PR65, $30) (PR66, $60-
$90) (PR68, $145-$375)
1961-D DDR (MS63, $10) (MS66, $50)
1963 DDO (PR64, $40) (PR65, $65) (PR66, $90) (PR67, $80-$85)
(PR69, $145)
1963 DDR (MS64, $75) (MS65, $20) (MS66, $155-$330) (PR64,
$30-$150) (PR65, $25-$210) (PR66, $30-$280) (PR67, $40-$375)
(PR68, $85-$710) (PR69, $110-$150) 2022
1963-D DDR (AU55, $10) (MS66, $90)
1964 DDR (MS65, $15) (PR67, $30)
1964-D DDO (MS65, $800-$1,840) (MS66, $280)
1964-D DDR (AU53, $50-$150) (AU55, $55-$60) (MS63, $160)
(MS64, $165-$1,150) (MS65, $95-$2,500) 2022
1968 DDO (MS65, $30) (MS67, $70-$75) (PR64, $25)
1968-S DDO (PR67 $50-$110) (PR68, $185)
1968-S DDR (PR64, $30) (PR65, $25) (PR67, $125)
1970-D DDR (MS64, $10-$80) (MS65, $10-$60) (MS66, $60-
$100)

Roosevelt Dimes
Filled Dies
1979-S filled S (PR70, $85-$425)
1981-S filled S (PR70, $105-$510)

Roosevelt Dimes
Fragments

1964-D reverse struck (MS64, $165-$170)
1965 (NG, $85-$90) 2022
1968-D 1gram (AU58, $140-$145) 2022
1991 w/brockage (MS63, $240)
No date (MS62, $175-$375) (MS64, $185) 2022
No date w/3 bonded pieces (MS63, $365)
No date w/flipover (MS63, $635)
No date w/flipover & double struck (MS63, $1,300) 2022
No date w/multi-struck (MS60, $155-$160)
No date w/ struck eight times (MS63, $375)

Roosevelt Dimes
Lamination
1961 (AU58, $35)
1963-D (XF40, 10)
1964-D (AU58, $20)
1965 (XF45, $10)
1967 (AU55, $50)

Roosevelt Dimes
Off center
1946 (MS64, $125)
1948-S (AU55, $170-$220)
1951 (MS62, $320)
1951-S (MS63, $405)
1954 (MS62, $70)
1955-S (MS65, $260)
1956-x (MS61, $115)
1957 (MS60, $55)
1962 (MS64, $140-$155)
1963 (MS62, $155)
1964 (MS60, $90) (MS61, $400) (MS62, $165) (MS63, $55-$190)
(MS64, $130-$165)
1964-D (MS60, $160) (MS66, $80)
1965 (MS60, $80)
1969-D (MS65, $430)

1970-D (MS66, $35)
1971 (MS60, $25)
1972-D (MS62, $160)
1973 (MS62, $90)
1977 (MS60, $70) (MS65, $35)
1978 (MS60, $25) (MS61, $240) (MS65, $15-$30)
1979-D (MS63, $90)
1983-D (MS61, $20)
1983-P (MS60, $35)
1988-D (MS63, $30)
1989-D (MS64, $30)
1989-P (MS63, $75) (MS65, $45)
1990-P (MS62, $70)
1991-P (MS62, $25) (MS63, $30) (MS65, $95)
1994-D (MS65, $5)
1994-P (MS65, $5)
1995-D (MS65, $75) (MS66, $60)
1995-P (MS64, $35-$55)
1996-P (MS60, $50) (MS63, $10) (MS65, $65)
1998-P (MS66, $20)
1999-P (MS62, $30) (MS63, $15-$20) (MS64, $15-$30) (MS65, $15-$25)
2000-P (MS63, $45) (MS64, $65) (MS65, $15-$65)
2007-P (MS63, $55)

Roosevelt Dimes
RPMs/Repunched date/Misplaced
1946-D D/D (MS66, $50)
1946-S S/S (MS62, $54) (MS63, $10-$25) (MS64, $25) (MS65 $30) (MS66, $70) 2022
1946-S S/S & DDR (AU53, $50-$105) (MS63, $10-$20) (MS64, $30-$140) (MS65, $30-$155) (MS66, $90-$95) (MS67, $540) (MS68, $2,760)
1946-S S/S/S/S (MS65, $40)
1946-S S/S/S/S & DDR (MS64, $40-$60)
1946-S S/S/S (MS64 $45-$60) (MS65, $40)

1946-S S/S/S & DDR (MS64, $30-$135) (MS65, $40)
1947-S S/D (VF30, $25) (MS64, $115) (MS65, $65) (MS66, $50-$165) 2022
1947-S S/D, w/trumpet S (MS64, $120)
1947-S S/S (MS66, $50-$85) 2022
1948-S S/S (MS64, $25) (MS66, $25-$50)
1949-S S/S (MS66, $30-$45) (MS67, $50)
1950-S S over inverted S (MS65, $65-$85) (MS67, $625)
1950-S S/D (MS65, $85-$110) (MS66, $160-$300)
1951 D/D (MS65, $50) (MS66, $175-$210)
1951-S S/S (MS66, $50)
1952-D D/D (MS66, $175)
1952-S S/S (MS66, $50)
1953-D D over horizontal D (MS64, $265) (MS66, $50) 2022
1953-S S/S (MS64, $20)
1954-S S/S (MS65, $40) (MS66, $80-$100) 2022
1955-D D/D (MS63, $10)
1959-D D/D (MS64, $30-$35) (MS65, $50) (MS66, $110)
1959-D D over inverted D (MS65, $40-$90) (MS66, $100)
1960-D/D (MS65, $150) (MS66, $130-$325) 2022
1962-D D over horizontal D (MS66, $150)
1964-D D/D (MS64, $35-$55) (MS66, $285) 2022
1968-S S/S (PR66, $425)
1969-D/D (MS64, $15-$30) (MS65, $10-$30) (MS66, $155)
1975-S S/S (PR69, $885)

Roosevelt Dimes
Split
1962-D before strike, obverse (AU58, $30)
1963-D planchet, obverse (MS62, $100)
1963-D planchet, reverse (MS65, $125)
1964 before strike, obverse (MS63, $60-$140)
1964-D before strike, obverse (no grade, $70-$100)
196x-D before strike, obverse (no grade, $45)
No date planchet, obverse (MS65, $125)
No date planchet, obverse, w/off center (no grade, $150)

No date planchet, reverse (MS64, $60)

Roosevelt Dimes
Striking Errors
1964 double strike, w/flip over & 50% off center (MS64, $1,610)
1964 triple struck (MS64, $635)
1964-D double struck, w/70% off center (MS61, $375)
1965 double struck, w/70% off center (MS61, $380)
1970 double struck, w/90% off center (MS62, $25-$80)
1970-D triple struck, w/saddle strike (MS66, $1,955)
1973 triple stuck, w/flip over (G, $1,035)
1973-S double struck (PS67, $1,800)
1974 double struck (MS60, $20)
1976 double struck, w/flip over (MS64, $425)
1976-D double struck (AU55, $35)
1976-D multiple struck (MS67, $150)
1977 die cap (MS69, $1,725)
1977-S double struck, w/off center (PR69, $2,100)
1979-D triple struck, w/flip over (MS64, $1495)
1981-P double struck, w/80% off center (MS60, $35)
1983-P chain struck, w/60% off center (MS63, $65) 2022
1985-P double struck (MS66, $180)
1986-P double struck (MS62, $85)
1988-P double struck, w/65%/95% off center (MS63, $130-$375)
1993-P brockage (MS63, $15)
1994-P chain struck (MS65, $10) 2022
1994-P double struck (MS63, $40)
1995 mule reverse of one cent (MS64, $58,000)
1996-P broadstruck, brockage (MS66, $35)
1996-P double struck (AU58, $2,100)
1998-P brockage (MS62, $25)
1999-P bonded (MS64, $1,725-$3,360) 2022
1999-P broadstruck (MS66, $50)
1999-P brockage (MS66, $35)
1999-P double struck (MS66, $485) (MS67, $920)
1999-D double struck (MS64, $60)

1999-x multiple struck (MS64, $2,300)
1999-x multiple struck & triple bonded (MS64, $2,000)
19xx bonded, w/multiple strikes (MS67, $600-$605) 2022
2000-P double struck (MS64, $25)
2001-P brockage, w/clashed dies (MS64, $80)
2001-P mated pair (MS65, $890)
No date bonded pair (MS65, $1,555-$3,125)
No date bonded, w/multiple strikes (MS63, $1,450) (MS65, $1,555)
No date broadstruck, w/brockage (MS63, $35) (MS65, $80)
No date double struck (MS63, $150) (MS64, $125-$1,380)
No date double struck, w/saddle struck (MS65, $155)
No date saddle struck (MS65, $80-$130)

Roosevelt Dimes
Tapered, Thin and Thick
1951-D thin (VF20, $50)
1951-S thin (VF20, $15)

Roosevelt Dimes
Variations
1954-S no "JS" designer initials (MS66, $165)
1964 blunt 9 (MS66, $20) 2022
1964 pointed 9 (MS66, $20) (PR68, $75) (PR69, $110-$400) 2022
1964-D blunt 9 (MS66, $20)
1968 proof no S (PR66, $10,575-$18,400) (PR67, $11,500-$37,375) (PR68, $10-$48,875) (PR69, $90) (PR70, $5,000) 2022
1969 reverse of 1968 (MS65, $50)
1970 proof no S (PR66, $440-$565) (PR67, $285-$1,100) (PR68, $600-$6,040) (PR69, $5,750-$6,000)
1970 reverse of 1968 (MS66, $50)
1970-D reverse of 1968 (MS66, $50-$90) 2022
1970-S no S (PR66, $555) (PR67, $450) 2022
1975 no S (PR68, $256,000) 2022
1981-S clear S (PR70, $100-$1,350)

1982 no P (AU58, $75) (MS64, $95-$175) (MS65, $110-$375) (MS66, $240-$480) (MS66FB, $340) (MS67, $290-$800) (MS68, $995-$2,185) 2022
1983 proof no S (PR66, $950) (PR67, $450-$1,000) (PR68, $450-$1,955) (PR69, $660-$1,955) (PR70, $15-$8,225) 2022

Roosevelt Dimes
Wrong US and Foreign Planchets
1964-D silver dime planchet (MS63, $1,265)
1965 silver dime planchet (AU55, $4,000-$8,625) (MS60, $1,815)
1973-S Liberia planchet (PR65, $1,380)
1998-P one cent planchet (MS64, $1,850-$4,450)
1999-D one cent planchet (MS65, $6,900)

Chapter Six – Photographs of Coin Errors

Buffalo Nickel Errors

Two feathers

1913 DDO

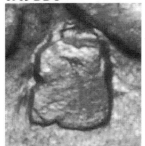

1913-S/S RPM

1915-D D/D

1916 DDO

1917 no "F" initial

1917 DDR

1918 8 over 7

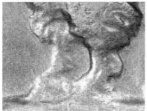
1926-D 3-1/2 legs

1927-D/D RPM

1929 DDO

1929-S/S RPM   1929-S/S/S RPM

1930 DDO

1930 DDR

1930-S DDO

1930-S/S RPM

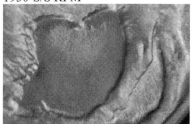
1931-S DDR

1931-S triple DDR

1934-D small D

1935 DDR

1935-D/D RPM   1935-D/D/D/D RPM

1935-S/S RPM

1936 DDO

1936-D/D RPM   1936-S/S RPM

1937-D/D RPM

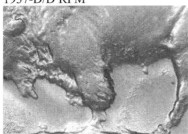

1937-D three leg

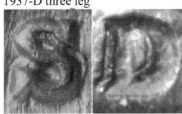

1937-S/S RPM   1938-D/D RPM

x

1938-D/S RPM   1938-D/D/D/S RPM

Jefferson Nickel Errors

1938 DDO

1938-D/D RPM

1939 reverse of 1938

1939 reverse of 1940[35]

1939 DDR

1941-D/D RPM

1940-S/S RPM

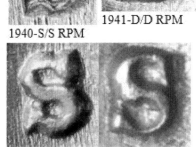

1941-S small and large "S"

---

[35] The reverse of 1940 is stronger and outlined.

1941-S/S RPM large "S"

1942 DDO

1942-D D/D horizontal "D" RPM   1942-D/D RPM

1942-S/S RPM

1942-P/P RPM   1942-P/P/P RPM

1943 DDO

1943-P/P RPM

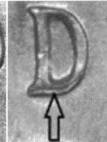

1943-P/P/P RPM   1943-D/D RPM

1943 3 over 2

1943-S/S RPM   1944-D/D RPM   1944-P/P RPM

1944-S/S RPM   1945-P/P RPM   1945-P/P/P RPM

1945-D/D RPM   1946-D/D RPM

1946 DDR

1946-S DDO

1946-D RPM   1946-D/D RPM 1949-D/S RPM
inverted "D"|

1951 DDO

1953 DDO

1953-D/D RPM   1954-D/D RPM   1954-S/D RPM
Inverted "D"

1955-D/S RPM

1956 DDO

1956 triple DDR

1960 quadruple DDR

1961 DDR

1962 DDR

1964-D D/D RPM

1964 DDR

1968-S S/S RPM

1975-D misplaced mintmark

1990-S DDO

2004-P DDO Handshake

2005-P peace metal DDO

2005-D speared bison[36]

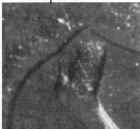

2005-D detached leg

Mercury Dime Errors

1919 DDO

1926 DDO

1929-S DDO

1931-S DDO

1934-D/D RPM   1935-S/S RPM

1936 DDO

1937 DDO

1937-D/D RPM   1938-D/D RPM

1939 DDO

1939-D/D RPM   1940-D/D RPM

1940-S/S RPM

1941 DDO

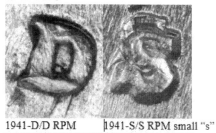

1941-D/D RPM   1941-S/S RPM small "s"

1942 Mercury dime 2 over 1

1942-D/D RPM   1943-D/D RPM

1943-S/S/S RPM   1943-S trumpet "S"

1944-D DDO

1944-D/D RPM

1945 DDO

1945-D/D RPM   1945-D/D horizonal "D"

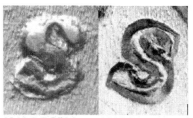

1945-S/S RPM   1945-S trumpet "S"

1945-S/S horizonal "S"

Roosevelt Dime Errors

1946 DDO/DDR

1946-D/D RPM   1946-S/S RPM

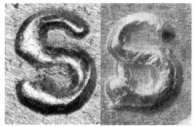

1946-S sans serif   1947-S/D sans serif letter

1947-S DDR

1948 DDR

1948-S/S RPM

1950-D DDR

1950-S/S RPM   1950-S inverted "S"

1951-D/D RPM   1951-S/S RPM

1952-S/S RPM   1953-D/D RPM

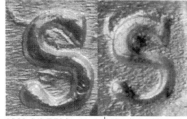

1953-S/S RPM   1954-S/S RPM

1954-S no "S"

1955-S/S RPM   1959-D inverted "D"

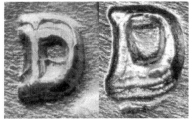

1959-D/D RPM   1960-D/D RPM

1962-D/D RPM   1963-D/D RPM

1963-D DDO

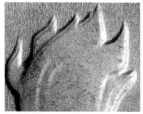

1963 DDR

1964 Blunt 9

1964 Pointed 9

1964-D/D RPM

1966 DDR

1968 DDO

1968-S/S RPM

1968-S DDO

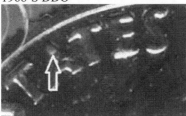
1968-S DDR

1969-D D/D RPM

1970-D DDR

1975-S S/S

The mint used the 1968 proof reverse die to mint coins for circulation in 1968, 1969, and 1970. Below are the photographs of the two die reverses. The most noticeable difference is in the lines in the torch with deeply grooved lines in the flame.

Normal reverse of a Roosevelt dime for circulation

Proof reverse of 1968

Appendix A - Doubled Die Classifications

Class I Doubled Die

When reworking a die to the hub, the die is slightly rotated to the left or right, doubling the letters and numbers. Class I doubled dies are like the 1955 and the 1969-S Lincoln cents with doubling.

Class II Doubled Die

Class two doubled die shows the strongest doubling toward the coin's rim or center. An example of this error is the 1971 DDO Lincoln cent.

Class III Doubled Die

When a die is impressed into a different working hub for the same mintage year, the results show a doubling in the die differences. In 1960, dies were producing large dates and small dates.

The 1960-D Lincoln cent above is a large over a small date.

Class IV Doubled Die

The doubled die occurs by a sequence of hubbing with an annealing process in between. The centers of the die and the hub are not aligned. Doubling is above all lettering and numbering on the coins. All coins dated 1998 and before using this process may have this error type.

1984 DDO Lincoln cent

Class V Doubled Die

Class V doubled die shows doubling to the right or the left around the coin with a widespread, into a medium spread, and finally a minor spread. For example, Liberty will have widespread doubling, the Motto will have a medium spread, and the date will have a minor spread.

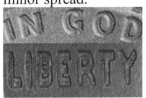

1995 DDO Lincoln cent

Class VI Doubled Die

Class six doubled die occurs when the coins' letters or numbers are thick and may even slope downward. The 2014 Lincoln cent pictured is a class a VI. The thickness of the numbers shown at the bottom of the photo with the overlap is apparent.

2014 DDO Lincoln cent

Class VII Doubled Die
Class VII doubled die results from a broken hub. The first impression on the die is from a standard hub, and a subsequent impression is from a broken hub. The Class VII doubled dies have been theorized, and no examples have been discovered.

Class VIII Doubled Die
A class eight doubled die occurs when the hub is tilted, and a working die is made from this hub. A slight doubling of letters shows a bump or a curve of raised material around the numbers and letters.

1939 DDO Lincoln cent

Glossary

Abrasions – Abrasions are scattered lines on the surface of a coin caused by scratches on the die.

Alloy – Mixture of metals in the sheet stock used for blanking planchets for the minting process.

Almost Uncirculated – A coin with minor wear on the highest points of the coin.

Annealing – Planchets are softened to enable details to be minted on coins. Metal rods are annealed to make Mint dies.

ANA – The American Numismatic Association is an organization dedicated to coin collecting.

ANACS – American Numismatic Association Certification Service

Anvil Die – The bottom die which creates the reverse on a coin.

Ball Serif – The top part of a S minted coin has a thick round ball.

Bar Die Break – A die break over the tops of the lettering on a coin appears like a bar.

Basining – The process of polishing dies before the minting process. Basining will cause some of the intended coin details to be flatter than the intended height.

BIE – A die break between the letters B and E in Liberty creates an irregular line of raised metal appearing like the letter I.

Blank – A raw planchet ready for striking.

BN – Abbreviation for brown

Bonded Pair – Two or more blanks enter the minting chamber struck together as one piece.

Burnishing – The process of polishing planchets before striking.

Brass Colored - Improper mixing of plating alloys creates a bronze or brass color on the surface of copper coins.

Broken Hub – A piece of the coin detail is missing from the hub, and consequently, the die made from the hub lacks the full detail.

Brilliant Uncirculated (BU) – A coin with no wear and has maintained the original mint luster.

Broadstruck – The collar holding the planchet for striking is cracked or missing creating a coin wider than usual.

Brockage - An early capped die impression where a sharp incused image has been left on the next coin fed into the coining chamber. Most brockages are partial; full brockages are rare and the most desirable form of the error.[37]

Broken Punch – A punch used to create a die is partially broken, resulting in missing details on a minted coin.

Business Strike – Coins minted for circulation.

CAC – Certified Acceptance Corporation

Cameo (CAM) – A proof or proof-like coin with a frosty appearance.

Canceled Planchet – A minted coin not meeting the Mint's standard is crushed in the shape of a waffle.

Chain Struck – Two planchets or a minted coin and a planchet enter the minting chamber and are struck with a portion of one over the other.

Carbon Spot – Oxidation on the coin's surface creates black spotting.

Choice Uncirculated – An alternative for using the mint state grading system. Choice Uncirculated coins are MS65.

Cleaned – A coin with an altered surface from using detergents, brushing, or any other chemical used to clean the surface.

Clashed Dies – Dies pressed together in the minting process with no planchet. Subsequent coins are minted with details from the opposite side appearing on the surface.

Clipped Planchet – A planchet blank missing part of the circumference. Clipped planchets vary in degree and type of error.

Clogged Die – Debris enters a die cavity resulting in the details on the coin not being raised to the specifications, partially or entirely missing.

Collar - A collar is a metal die that positions a planchet between the dies, so the coin is minted as intended. Collars are considered the "third" die and are used to impart the edge markings.

---

[37] PCGS – PCGS website "Lingo"

Collar Break Vertical - When the collar cracks vertically, the coins minted show the lettering and numbers butted against the rim.

Collar Clash - A collar clash occurs when the striking die is not lined up correctly, and the die strikes the collar. The features on the collar, sometimes a reeded edge, are transferred to the die and appear on coins minted.

Collar Vibration - During the coin striking, the collar vibrates, the hammer die pushes the coin down toward the anvil die, creating a sloping outer ridge toward the center of the coin.

Contact Marks - Nicks, and dents on coins from other coins or foreign objects.

Corrosion – Damage to a coin caused by the environment or chemicals applied to the surface.

Counter Brockage - A previously struck coin and capped die is a counter brockage. The capped die strikes a coin already struck, and the obverse design is impressed into the cap. The result will be a design where the cap face will be an incuse.

Counterstamp - A coin stamped by a second source makes an intentional impression on the coin.

Counting Wheel Mark - A circular mark appears on the surface of a coin from a counting machine.

DCAM – Deep cameo coin

Denomination - The face value of a coin or bill.

Die - A die is a punch that contains the design used to imprint on a planchet creating a minted coin.

Defective Planchet - A defective planchet refers to a blank which was split, cracked, or missing pieces before the coining process.

Design – The mint impresses a metal rod under pressure into a hub to create a die for minting coins.

Die Adjustment Error – The pressure used to Mint a coin is adjusted, resulting in faint details.

Die Break – An area on the coin created by a broken die. Cuds are created from die breaks.

Die Cap - The term applied to an error in which a coin gets jammed in the coining press and remains for successive strikes, eventually forming a "cap" either on the upper or lower die. These are sometimes spectacular, with the "cap" often many times taller than a standard coin.[38]

Die Clash – Coins produced with dies that have impressions of the opposite sides of the design.

Die Crack – A crack in the die results in a raised metal line that could branch out on a coin's surface.

Die Cud – An area of raised smooth metal around the rim caused by a die piece that has broken away.

Die Cud Retained – A retained cud occurs when a piece of the die breaks but is held in place by the collar.

Die Errors – Coins minted from dies that are damaged or errantly modified by Mint workers

Die Gouges - The material in short, thick, raised lines or bumps on the surface of a coin caused by damage to the dies.

Die Scratches (see Abrasions) - A series of raised lines on a coin's surface from debris or die tooling.

Die Wear – Overuse of a die, causing the design details to be weakly struck.

DDO – Doubled die obverse

DDR –Doubled die reverse.

DMM – Doubled mintmark.

Doubled Die – A distinct doubling of the design on a coin created from dies doubled from the hub.

Doubled Rim – Die misalignment and the failure to strike the planchet upset rim leaves the upset rim and creates a second rim.

Double-Struck – A coin trapped in the collar struck a second time.

Environmental Damage - Damage to a coin's surface is caused by pollutants.

Extended Rim - An extended rim occurs with a deep strike on the coin. Slight tilting the coin during the minting process creates a thin rim with a groove inside the rim.

Fasces - The reverse of a Mercury dime has a bundle of wood with an ax attached, described as a "fasces".

---

[38] PCGS – PCGS website "Lingo"

FB – Full bands – The designation for Mercury dimes with complete uninterrupted lies on the faces.

FBL – Full bell lines – The designation for Franklin halves with complete line detail on the Liberty bell.

FH – Standing liberty quarters with full details on the head of the portrait. PCGS defines full head as:

"Type I Standing Liberty Quarters earn the FH designation when there is a clear and distinct separation between Miss Liberty's hair cords and her cap.

Type II Standing Liberty Quarters receive the Full Head designation when the helmet exhibits three complete and distinct leaves, a complete outline on the bottom of the helmet, and a clear ear hole on Miss Liberty's head."

Filled Dies – Dies that become filled with debris blocking the design details from being transferred to the coin.

Finned Rim – A coin minted with an extended rim missing metal fill. The fin on the rim is thin and extends part of the way around the coin.

First Strike – Coins minted early at a mint and released to circulation are deemed "early strikes."

Flip-Over Strike – A coin jammed in the minting chamber is struck, flips over, and struck again with the opposite die.

Fold Over Strike – A coin not fully ejected in the minting chamber is struck again, crushing the coin.

Foreign Planchet – A planchet intended for mintages of a Foreign county.

Flow lines – Lines on the coin's surface caused by the metal spreading during striking.

Fragment – A small piece of a planchet in various shapes and sizes

FS – Full step designation for Jefferson nickels

Gem BU - A high-grade coin is regarded as MS67 that dealers and collectors use in place of the MS grading scale.

Hammer Die – The die used to Mint the obverse design.

Hub – The punch used to create the design dies for minting coins. The design is the opposite of the actual image.

Hub Error – When a hub piece breaks off, the dies created from the hub are missing the detail.

Improperly Annealed – Planchets that are not softened adequately for minting. The minted coins often appear with a red tint.

Indent – Another planchet enters the minting chamber and crushes into the minted coin, creating a deep impression.

Inverted Mintmark - A mintmark placed on a working die upside down.

Key Coin – The most valuable coin in a series

Lamination – A defective planchet is minted, and then the defective portion falls away.

Lamination Retained – The defective portion of the coin peels from the coin's surface but remains on the coin.

Large Date – A coin release for a date with at least two different date sizes, one which is considered larger.

Machined Doubled – The striking die bounces slightly during the strike creating a thin raised area around the letters or numbers.

Master Die – A die produced from the original hub.

Master Hub – A hub produced from a rubber mold design on metal hardened used to make minting dies.

Mated Pairs – Two planchets struck together in error. The coins are separate and are boxed in the same container. The two separate coins are located as a pair.

Mintmark: The mintmark is a letter on most coins representing where the coins were minted.

D – Denver

S – San Francisco

P – Philadelphia (also no mintmark)

W – West Point

CC – Carson City

O – New Orleans

Mint State – A coin that has no wear.

Mint Striking Errors – Errors created in the minting process.

Misaligned Dies - There are three dies, the hammer, the anvil, and the collar, designed to mint coins as intended. When the dies are not aligned correctly, the strike on the coin is not centered.

Missing Details – Part of the design is not transferred to the coin properly.

Mistruct - A coin that has been minted with a broken collar or misaligned dies.

Motto – The inscription on a coin such as "IN GOD WE TRUST."

MPD - The date is incorrectly positioned on the die and is misplaced on minted coins.

MS – Mint state grading system MS60 through MS70.

Mule – A mule is a coin minted with two different denominations on opposite sides.

Multiple Struck – A coin trapped in the collar and struck several times.

NG - no grade – A coin with significant damage or other issues is not graded by a third party grading service.

Numismatist – A person who studies and accumulates knowledge of money.

Obverse – The front of a coin

Occluded Gas – Bubbles appear on the coin's surface caused by gas trapped during plating.

Off Center – A coin struck on a blank that was not correctly centered over the anvil, or lower, die.[39]

OMM – Over mintmark - A coin struck with a die repurposed with a different mintmark.

Overdate – A coin minted with a date that has been partially removed and replaced by another date.

Partial Collar – A planchet fed into the minting chamber is struck outside the collar.

Partial Collar Tilted - A coin entering the minting chamber struck on an angle with a cracked or moving collar.

PCGS – Professional Grading Service

---

[39] PCGS – PCGS website "Lingo"

Phantom Mintmark – A mintmark not completely removed from a die faintly shows on coins.

PL – Proof-like – A coin minted for circulation but with dies that may have been used for minting-proof coins.

Planchet – The blank used to mint coins.

PR – Proof – A coin minted by the US Mint with highly polished and maintained dies.

Ragged – A numismatic term for a planchet which is missing a piece of the planchet in an irregular shape.

RB – Red Brown color

Raw – A term used to describe a coin that is not graded.

Relief – The intended design height on a coin.

Reverse Brockage - Similar brockage but with the portrait facing the opposite way.

Retained Collar Cud – The collar breaks in the minting process but does not split apart, resulting in an incomplete rim.

Rotated – Dies not aligned correctly, minting coins with the obverse and reverse not lined up correctly.

Rotated Mintmark – A mintmark placed on a die in a usual position.

RPD – Repunched date. The date was modified on the original die to strenthen the details

RPM – The attempt to remove and replace a mintmark creates an error when not all of the first mintmark is removed.

Saddle Strike – Saddle struck coins occur in a multi-press operation when the coin straddles two presses. Both presses stamp the coin while the coin bends between the dies in the shape of a saddle.

Sandwich Coin – The interior of a coin is one alloy covered by another alloy on both sides. Modern-day silver coins contain copper interiors with silver plating on both sides.

Slab – A slag term used for third party grading of coins encapsulated.

SMS – Special mint set

SP – Proof-like Specimen labeled on NGC holders

Split Planchet – A planchet missing a portion of metal on the surface.

Spread – The degree of doubling on a coin. Spreads are high, medium, and low.

Strike Through – Debris entering the minting chamber distorts the intended details on the coin.

Thick or Thin Planchet – All US denominations have tolerances for the coin's thickness. When a planchet is thin or thick, the coin becomes lighter or heavier than intended.

Tilted Collar - A tilted collar strike occurs when a planchet enters the minting chamber at an angle and is struck by the hammer die pushing the coin flat. The result of this strike is a smooth outer surface lacking detail. There are varying degrees of part of the coin's circumference missing details.

Tilted Mintmark – A mintmark hammered into a die at an angle, leaving the details thick on one side and thin on the other side.

Tooling Mark - Raised areas on a coin are not intended as part of the design but are from reworking the dies.

Transitional – Coins struck with planchets not intended for a subsequent mintage. For example, a 1943 Lincoln cent struck on a bronze planchet. A 1983 Lincoln cent struck on a bronze planchet (no- zinc) is a transitional error.

Type one – The first intended issuance of a coin. For example, in 1913, Buffalo nickel on a raised mound.

Type two – The Mint modified the design during the annual mintage of coins. The 1913 Buffalo nickel struck with a flat mound is a type II mintage.

Uniface - A coin planchet enters the minting chamber over a planchet already in the minting chamber. The planchets struck together, leaving one side blank and the other with the intended details.

Unplated – A coin missing the plating layer exposing the inner core.

VAM – A numbering system created for silver dollar variations. VAM is short for Van Allen and Mallis, the two people who logged silver dollar variances.

Variations - Variations are not mint errors in the technical sense. Differences in coins caused by creating hubs used to create dies that are not identical.

Variety – Changes in the design of a coin during a minting year produce coins with different features such as a large S or a small s.

Vertical Collar Break – A collar breaks vertically during minting, giving the coin a doubled rim.

Weakly Struck – Missing or lightly struck details due to worn or clogged dies.

Wheel marks – Faint, highly polished lines on a coin caused by the rubber wheels in counting machines.

Whizzing – A process of using high-pressure water and brushes to clean the surface of a coin noted as whizzing.

Wood-Grained – The coin shows lines across the coin's surface caused by toning or an improper alloy mix.

Wrong Metal – A metal alloy unintentionally used for the minting of coins such as brass.

Wrong Planchet – A planchet not intended for the mintage, such as a dime planchet minted in Lincoln cent dies.

1J

About the Author

I started collecting coins in 1962, and my passion for collecting has continued to grow, expanding with error coins in the 1990s.

The 1960s

In 1963, finding a 1909 VDB Lincoln cent was my inspiration for collecting. I was intrigued by the date and the large letters on the reverse of the coin, VDB. Before long, I purchased the Whitman blue folders for Lincoln cents and began to search for the dates and mint-marked coins I could find. I bought all types of books and magazines to learn as much as I could about coins. These books helped me become an expert and enabled me to grade coins, even those I sent for encapsulation correctly. My encapsulated coins have always come back as MS65 or higher, and I could not expect more.

During the 1960s, collecting from circulation was fun since many types and types of coins were available. Back in the 1960s, there were Lincoln cents dated from 1909, Buffalo nickels, Mercury dimes, Standing Liberty quarters, and Walking Liberty half dollars. Some silver dollars circulated. The rarest coin from circulation I saw was a 1916-D Mercury Dime. My friend and I would search through coin rolls together in the early 1960s. We agreed to share our finds as we pooled our cash. Unfortunately, the thought of more money got the best of him, and he refused to share the profits.

In the 1960s, the best method I determined for searching for dates I needed to fill my collection was to go to the local bank and obtain Lincoln cent rolls. After a year, I was able to fill the Lincoln cent folder from 1909 through 1963 will most of the coins. The only coins I was missing were most of the mint marked Lincoln cents dated before 1916. I had located higher-end Lincoln cents for 1909, 1909 VDB, 1910, 1911, 1912, 1913, 1914, and 1915. I completed the

Lincoln set from 1916, except for 1922, 1931-S, 1932, 1932-D, 1933, and 1933-D Lincoln cents. Lincoln cents with the San Francisco mint mark "S" were getting hard to locate in the early nineteen sixties.

The 1970s

By the 1970s, "S" minted coins were near impossible to find. The return of San Francisco coins for circulation in 1968 was by popular demand. The mint issued the "S" dated coins from 1968 through 1974 for circulation. Since that time, the mint has used the San Francisco mint for proof sets.

Most silver coins had vanished from circulation in the 1970s, leaving almost nothing to collect from circulation except for Jefferson nickels. By this time, most of the wheat cents disappeared from hoarding.

During the 1970s, I shelved my collection since there was virtually nothing to acquire from circulation.

The 1980s

In the 1980s, nothing had changed with collecting coins from circulation. The clad coinage was in circulation since 1965, but the mystique of collecting was gone. Jefferson nickels dated before 1965 were becoming scarce.

The 1990s

I have never been able to locate the coins I was missing for my collection in circulation. I resorted to buying the coins I was missing to complete the sets in the 1990s. It was in the 1990s when I established SMCcoins LLC and began to sell online with a website. I attended every coin auction and estate sale to obtain coins to sell or add to my collection. In 1999, I gave up the site.

The 2000s

By 2000, I turned my attention to error coin collecting, and I wrote my first coin guide of error coins in 2000, inspired by the increasing numbers of error coins offered at auctions.

We search through thousands of Lincoln cents to provide accurate information for the error coin guides. We do locate some error coins which we either give away or sell for a modest price.

I still meet people who have coins they want to be appraised or sold. I do not buy collections, but I do sell the coins for them. The most extensive collection I have ever sold was for $30,000.

I hope you enjoy this book. If you have any questions, contact me at errorcoinexpert@aol.com

Books are written and offered by Stan McDonald
2023 US Error Coin Guide
2023 US Error Coin Guide – color edition
2023 Lincoln Cent Error Coin Guide
2023 Lincoln Cent Error Coin Guide – color edition
2023 Lincoln Cent Error Searching Guide: 150,000 Coins Searched
2023 Lincoln Cent Mint State Price Guide
2023 Jefferson Nickel and Roosevelt Dime Error Coin Guide
2023US Error Coin Guide – Novice Edition
2023 Lincoln Cent Design and Profile Guide

References
Photographs are from the personal collection of the author, photographed at auctions, or validated pictures from the internet. Error type descriptions are from years of collecting experience, and interpretation validated by the PCGS.
PCGS – As noted in this guide by footnotes.

The U.S. Treasury Department – As footnoted in this guide.
[4B]

Made in United States
Orlando, FL
28 January 2023

29164176R00087